DOING BUSINESS IN GERMANY

DOING BUSINESS IN GERMANY

A LEGAL MANUAL

BY

Dr. RUDOLF MUELLER
FRANKFURT/MAIN
RECHTSANWALT UND NOTAR

Dr. ERNST STIEFEL
NEW YORK
MEMBER OF THE NEW YORK BAR
MEMBER OF THE GERMAN BAR

Dr. HORST BRÜCHER
FRANKFURT/MAIN
RECHTSANWALT UND NOTAR

8th fully revised edition

1978

FRANKFURT AM MAIN FRITZ KNAPP VERLAG

CIP-Kurztitelaufnahme der Deutschen Bibliothek

Mueller, Rudolf
Doing business in Germany: a legal manual / by Rudolf Mueller; Ernst
Stiefel; Horst Brücher. – 8., fully rev. ed. – Frankfurt am Main: Knapp,
1978.
NE: Stiefel, Ernst; Brücher, Horst
ISBN 3 7819 0196-3

Copyright 1978 by Fritz Knapp Verlag, Frankfurt am Main
Gesamtherstellung: H. G. Gachet & Co., 6070 Langen
Printed in Germany

TABLE OF CONTENTS

The 8th Edition

In line with its long established record this legal manual shall continue to serve as a practical reader of German law for the foreign businessman who wishes to operate or invest in the Federal Republic of Germany, and for his legal advisors. In addition, this book will serve those who deal with Germans and German firms investing in foreign countries, a fast growing business since the early seventies, primarily in the United States of America and Canada. Understanding the German mind and its legal climate – "as they see it" – has become an important and useful element for the foreign parties involved in the initiation, negotiation, closing and continued success of those transatlantic ventures.

An extensive and detailed revision of this book again became necessary:

Since the 7th edition major developments occurred in the areas of cartel-antitrust law (mainly by the introduction of merger control), of tax law (mainly by a relief of double taxation of the profit of corporations), and of labor law (codetermination of labor in the supervisory boards of large corporations). In many other fields, the development of the law by international treaties, by domestic legislation, by the courts and also by voluntary arrangements within business has been lively in the past years. The emphasis is, and continues to be, on more protection of the private consumer and of labor under the otherwise maintained principles of the market economy: more security for the consumer and private parties against certain clauses in contract forms (general terms and conditions), for employee's and pensioner's rights in cases of insolvency of the firm, for depositors in the case of insolvency of banks.

In spite of ever pressing efforts of the European Commission, European law and the harmonization of certain regulations of the national laws of the EEC member states have made some but small progress only over the last years. The European regulations applying directly to business enterprises and nationals of the member states, the relative law, practices and trends are reported in this book in connection with the various applicable subjects. The European Community, after the entry in 1972 of Great-Britain, Ireland and Denmark, is still expected to grow by the entry of Greece, Portugal and Spain. Apart from other serious problems of such growth, the objective of the Rome Treaty of securing and enforcing free trade and competition and of harmonizing certain national laws will become still more difficult to achieve.

An almost secular event in its special field was the depositing of ratification records in 1977 by a number of the signatory states sufficient to render them effective: The European Patent Convention (which is not limited to the EEC member states) and the worldwide Patent Cooperation Treaty (PCT), including uniform rules on patent classification. The conventions provide for simplified patent applications within and outside of Europe; the substantive national patent laws have also considerably been harmonized. The German Patent Law has been amended to meet these requirements.

Another ambitious scholarly effort since the early thirties to harmonize the national laws in the important field of international sales resulted in the ratification by Germany and other states of the International Convention relating to the International Sale of Goods. But the convention permits too many reservations and will hardly become a practical feature of international trade.

As before, this manual reflects the practice of our specialized profession. We are thankful for the expert review and suggestions of the partners of Mueller and Brücher.

May 1978

Rudolf Mueller	Ernst Stiefel	Horst Brücher
Frankfurt/Main	New York	Frankfurt/Main

I. GERMAN LAW AND ITS INTERPRETATION

GENERAL

The law of Germany is as detailed, voluminous and complex as the body of law of any other civilized and industrialized community. Legal terminology and regulatory technique are highly developed and as uniform and abstract as feasible. The selection and presentation of law for the purposes of this manual have, therefore, obvious limitations. It should also be realized that the differences in the system or in the substance of any two bodies of law are easier to explain and to understand than the equally important differences of technique, construction and legal approach to facts. There remains the problem of language. The mere translation of a legal definition or a statute into another language may be inadequate for an understanding of the full meaning of the definition or statute – it may even be misleading.

SOURCES OF LAW

Germany is a so-called civil law country since the main body of its private law rules has been adapted from Roman law. This does not, however, apply to the wide field of established commercial and modern business law. Most German law is contained in general codes or special statutes. The major code in the field of civil law is the *Bürgerliche Gesetzbuch (BGB)* and of commercial law the *Handelsgesetzbuch (HGB)*.
Most German law is federal law. State law is practically limited to special fields of public law such as water rights, forestry, mining – including the regulation of the mining corporation (a federal mining law is proposed). State law regulates also foundations of private law and the constitution of state banks *(Landesbanken)*, the latter being subject to federal banking law. In addition state law simply supplements certain federal statutes.

INTERPRETATION

of statutory provisions is broad, not formal. While the statute as promulgated is decisive and is irrespective of legislative motives which have found no expression in the statute itself, the judge looks to the purpose of the statute as distinguished from a mere technical interpretation of its wording. Legal reasoning is deductive rather than inductive. Jurisprudence, i. e. legal doctrine in treatises or legal periodicals and in commentaries to codes and statutes, is rather influential upon courts. The system of commentaries in the form of extensive annotations to statutes is well developed. Commentaries explain the meaning of the individual statutory provisions in their context and recite and deal with applicable precedent and legal doctrine. Much of the law is judge-made. Such case law has been and is currently developed mainly to refine statutory definitions, particularly in areas where social and economic conditions or social values have changed and statutory regulation has been either missing or inadequate. Except for decisions of the Federal Constitutional Court, precedent is not binding upon a court. It is, however, normally followed.

THE STATUS OF ALIENS

As a general rule of German law German nationals and foreigners receive equal legal treatment. A number of legal issues, however, require special provisions for foreigners in both public and private law, so-called *Fremdenrecht*. The Law on Foreigners (*Ausländergesetz*) – in spite of its comprehensive title – is not a codification of the *Fremdenrecht* but merely regulates the admission and stay of foreigners in Germany. Nationals of the member states of the European Community enjoy free mobility including the right to accept employment in other member states. Some bilateral agreements as the Friendship Treaty of 1954 of Germany with the United States of America especially recognize equal treatment of the other nation's citizens. The classic definition of the foreigner by nationality is still applicable in regard to some constitutional rights or other public law and to some rules of private international law. But the definition of the foreigner by domicile or residence, irrespective of nationality, has become increasingly important in many fields in addition to tax-, customs- or foreign exchange regulations.

10

INTERNATIONAL TREATIES

The German constitution decrees that the recognized rules of international law form part of German federal law. Ratified treaties constitute German law. German economic and social policy favors the free international movement of capital, goods and labor and furthers the legal preconditions and consequences of the integration of the national economies, particularly in Europe. On the European continent, a similarity of legal systems and a greater willingness to sacrifice sovereignty permits or simplifies such efforts. As will be seen throughout this manual, Germany participates in the efforts to facilitate judicial, administrative and legal cooperation between nations.

II. COURTS, REGISTERS, OFFICIAL GAZETTES

THE COURTS

for civil, commercial and criminal matters constitute the regular court system. They are courts of general jurisdiction. In addition, administrative, tax, labor and social insurance matters are each subject to special court systems and cannot be brought before courts of general jurisdiction. All decisions by governmental agencies are as a matter of principle appealable to a court, generally the administrative court, unless a special regulation exists. The decisions of the Federal Cartel Office are appealable to the regular court at its Berlin domicile, an *Oberlandesgericht*, called the *Kammergericht*. The decisions of the federal Patent Office are appealable to a special Federal Patent Court at its Munich domicile. This court deals also with the revocation of patents and the granting of compulsory licenses under the Patent Law.
Both the regular and the special systems are separate national court systems. There are no concurrent federal and state courts.
In addition, a Federal Constitutional Court and constitutional courts of the states exist. To insure the uniformity of decisions of the various supreme courts, a Joint Senate of these courts has been established.

Except for petty cases which are decided by the local *Amtsgericht*, civil and commercial litigation is heard in the first instance before the regional *Landgericht*. An appeal on questions of both law and facts, together with the right to introduce new facts, goes to a superior court, the *Oberlandesgericht*. A further appeal, on questions of law only, may be made to the Federal Supreme Court, the *Bundesgerichtshof*. All these courts operate in several divisions. There are specialized divisions in some fields of law, for example unfair competition, restraint of trade, patent infringement, and in certain commercial cases.

REGISTERS

There are two court registers of general importance, the Title Register and the Commercial Register.

The Title Register *(Grundbuch)* indicates the rights and encumbrances of real estate and protects reliance in good faith on the entries. There is, therefore, no room for the business of title insurance. Title to real estate passes, and mortgages and land charges become effective only with the entry into the register.

The Commercial Register *(Handelsregister)* records certain data of merchants and commercial enterprises for the benefit of the public. Entry into this register has in some cases a constitutive effect – a corporation, for instance, comes into legal existence only with the entry of its formation data into the register. The appointment of corporate officers, on the other hand, is effective with the appointment, and is not dependent upon the subsequent registration.

Both registers are kept by the local court, the *Amtsgericht*, which as to the Commercial Register is called the Court of Register *(Registergericht)*. The decisions are appealable to the higher courts.

Some local courts maintain registers for ships, and the *Amtsgericht* in Braunschweig maintains the federal register for aircraft. The court registers show rights in such property. Administrative or quasi-judicial bodies keep registers or records – for example, the federal Patent Office for patents, utility models, trademarks and literary authors, and the Federal Cartel

Office for permitted cartel arrangements. There is no register for chattel mortgages.

OFFICIAL GAZETTES

Federal and state legislation is published in official gazettes. Federal law is contained in the Federal Legal Gazette *(Bundesgesetzblatt)*, formerly the *Reichsgesetzblatt*. The publications also show those implementing ordinances which are enacted by the government as a result of statutory delegation of legislative power. A second part of the *Bundes-(Reichs-) gesetzblatt* contains material such as ratified international treaties and conventions. The Federal Tax Gazette *(Bundessteuerblatt)* republishes all tax laws. It also contains ministerial directives for tax administration issued to the federal and state authorities, and the decisions and opinions of the Federal Fiscal Court *(Bundesfinanzhof)*. Similar data for customs and tariffs may be found in the Federal Customs Gazette *(Bundeszollblatt)*. The federal ministries and some federal agencies, such as the federal Patent Office, issue special gazettes to announce those administrative activities which are of interest to the public. The state governments issue their own legal gazettes.

Another federal gazette, the *Bundesanzeiger*, is used for the publication of major administrative decrees, directives, ordinances and decisions, and also for notices in the field of diplomatic and consular representation. It is also prescribed for officially required financial and other notices of companies.

III. JUDGES, ATTORNEYS, NOTARIES

JUDGES

of ordinary courts are generally appointed for life. Laymen serve in commercial matters before the *Landgericht* and in labor matters before the labor courts as associate judges for a limited term. In such cases – as in any other court where more than one judge hears the case – the judges consult jointly and decide by simple majority on both facts and law.

ATTORNEYS

In civil and commercial cases before the *Landgericht* or *Oberlandesgericht* the parties must be represented by attorneys who are admitted to such courts. The admission of attorneys to the *Landgericht* or *Oberlandesgericht* is restricted to the court competent for the district where the attorneys have their offices. Admission to the Federal Supreme Court is limited to a small number of attorneys. All attorneys may appear before the *Amtsgericht* and the administrative, penal, tax, labour and social courts. The legal profession is not divided into barristers and solicitors. The ethical conduct of attorneys is subject to the supervision of special courts of the profession *(Ehrengerichte)*. Detailed regulations exist with regard to the permissibility of giving professional advice in legal, tax and foreign exchange matters. A profession of "law agents" as in Great Britain does not exist.

NOTARIES

are not only authorized to certify signatures. They must be qualified lawyers. In some of the German states or regions, the notary is a special profession. In other areas senior attorneys are commissioned to act as notaries. The notaries have the responsibility for the validity of certain categories of transactions which require a full record before a notary in order to be valid and enforceable. This applies, for example, to transactions in the field of real estate and to certain corporate matters such as the formation of corporations or the preparation of the minutes of all shareholders' meetings of stock corporations and the assignment of *GmbH* shares. The notaries are authorized to act only in the district for which they are commissioned, but their acts carry unlimited authority within Germany, and abroad upon proper legalization of the notary's signature. A foreign noatary's signature is legalized for recognition in Germany, as a rule, by the German diplomatic or consular service. A Hague convention (among the members are the Federal Republic of Germany, the Netherlands, Switzerland and Great Britain) permits the legalization to be effected by an authority of the

14

notary's home state (apostille). Under some bilateral conventions no legalization of the foreign notary's signature is required (conventions between the Federal Republic of Germany, Denmark, France and Italy).

FEES

of attorneys and notaries are prescribed in detail by statutes. They follow, in principle, the litigation or transaction values. Notary fees cannot be altered by agreement. Attorneys, however, may – to some extent – agree on fees with due consideration of the statutory fees and canons of ethics. Fees contingent upon the outcome of a case and the splitting of fees are illegal.

IV. JURISDICTION, PROCEDURE, ARBITRATION

INTERNATIONAL AGREEMENTS

The German Federal Republic is a party to major multilateral treaties which facilitate international cooperation in court and arbitration matters – the Hague Convention on Civil Procedure (1905/1954), the Geneva Protocol on Arbitration Clauses (1923), the Geneva Convention on the Enforcement of Foreign Arbitration Awards (1927), the UN-Convention on the Recognition and Enforcement of Foreign Arbitral Awards (1958) and the Geneva European Convention on International Commercial Arbitration (1961). The Hague Convention on Civil Procedure has been amended by bilateral treaties between Germany and a number of states. Special bilateral arbitration conventions exist. Great Britain and the United States have joined the UN-Convention of 1958. Both countries, however, have concluded limited agreements with Germany. A German-British Agreement (1928) has been adhered to by Australia, Canada and New Zealand. Another special agreement was made in 1960 with Great Britain on the mutual recognition and enforcement of civil and commercial court decrees. With respect to the United States, the German-American Treaty

15

of Friendship, Commerce and Navigation (1954) provides for free access to and equal treatment before courts, the recognition of arbitration agreements and the recognition and enforcement of awards. Whereas the German-British agreements include judicial service, there is no German-American agreement on that question. Judicial assistance between American and German courts is entirely a matter of comity. A German court may agree to serve documents and to take evidence as requested by an American court, but the German court cannot force a person under its jurisdiction to appear as witness and to accept service, i. e. the person may refuse to do so.

Since February 1, 1973 there is in effect, as a major achievement, a fully workable multilateral convention of the European "Six" on the International Jurisdiction of Courts and the Execution of Judicial Decisions in Civil and Commercial Cases.

JURISDICTON AND VENUE

Jurisdiction in German courts is not predicated upon personal service. Constructive service is widely permitted. Personal evasion of process is not possible. Service of process upon foreign nationals, residents or enterprises with respect to proceedings pending before a German court is effected either through the appropriate authority in the foreign country or the German consular representative in that country. Except for a number of special cases

venue

is determined by the defendant's residence or place of business. Failing such residence in Germany, venue is determined at the place where the defendant holds property of any nature regardless how trifling its value; no prior attachment of such property is needed nor is the enforcement of a resulting judgment limited to such property. This rather disturbing venue has been eliminated between the European "Six" by the 1973 Convention on the International Jurisdiction. The place of performance of a contract also constitutes a place of venue. As to tort, including infringement of patents, any place where the

16

tortious act was committed may be selected by the plaintiff. The doctrine of "forum non conveniens" is not part of German law. Jurisdiction of a court may also be established by express or implied consent of the parties; it is quite common to include jurisdictional clauses in contracts or general business conditions; printed forms suffice if they are permissible under general rules of law. Such consent or stipulation, however, is invalid independent of the applicable law if only one party to it does not have the status of a merchant. "Private" parties may be sued only in the courts of their residence or of the place of performance. If the proper law of a contract between merchants is foreign law, the latter decides whether or not a venue clause in the general business conditions is valid. In international trade it is sometimes questionable whether or not such clauses are meant to be exclusive or optional only for one or both of the parties. Agreements on the jurisdiction of a certain (foreign) court may still be disregarded if they constitute an abuse; for example, if they are designed either to avoid enforcement in Germany or to take advantage of the superior financial or economic position of one of the contracting parties.

The question of jurisdiction must be decided by the court ex officio. The question of venue, however, will be decided only if the defendant raises an objection or if an exclusive statutory rule exists. There is no requirement of a "special appearance" if the defendant wishes to contest the court's jurisdiction. If the court finds that it has no jurisdiction or venue, it must, on motion of plaintiff, refer the case to the proper court.

With jurisdiction as with substantive legislation, the governing principle is that foreign nationals be granted the same legal protection as German nationals. Only when a foreign country discriminates against German nationals may reprisals be adopted in the jurisdictional sphere.

CAPACITY TO SUE

Every person with a general capacity to contract or to acquire and perform duties, i. e. possessing legal capacity, is also competent to act as a party to a suit or other legal proceeding. A foreign (or domestic) association or entity without such capacity under its own law which acts in business de facto may, however, be sued in Germany.

Foreign nationals or residents may, however, act as parties to suits and other legal proceedings if they possess that capacity according to the applicable foreign law. Thus the partnership or the trust, as known in Anglo-American law, is competent to appear before German courts as a party to legal proceedings. The branch of a foreign firm in Germany enjoys the same capacity as the foreign firm does abroad. A German court will refer to foreign law to determine capacity in this situation.

ACTIONS AND PLEADINGS

In German law there is no formal distinction between actions as there is in English and American law. Also there is no distinction between actions at law and actions in equity. In general, there are three types of complaint in court – the action for specific performance which includes restraining the defendant from committing an act, the action for damages, both *Leistungsklagen*, and the action to determine a legal situation, *Feststellungsklage*. A cause of action may be changed without formal amendment of the pleadings. While great emphasis is placed on the briefs, pleadings are in no way technical. Changes and amendments are liberally allowed as long as they do not basically change the subject matter of the suit and merely assert the same claim in a different form. The court may, however, refuse to recognize procedural actions or omissions of a party which intentionally or negligently delay the proceedings.

THE ORAL HEARING (TRIAL)

is mandatory for court procedure. Several hearings on the same case in the trial courts are common. The parties may, however, waive the hearing. Preliminary injunctions, temporary restraining orders or seizures may be granted in case of urgency without a hearing with the full risk upon the applicant. The judge plays a dominant role in the proceedings. He directs proceedings, takes the

18

evidence

and usually formulates in his language the record made of the hearing. The court must warn parties of points they may have overlooked. Procedure is rather informal. This applies also to the rules of evidence. There is no time limit to oral presentations. Except before the Federal Supreme Court, such presentations are seldom complete. Rather, they amend, emphasize or clarify points in the briefs at the suggestion of the court. Every

judgment

must be in writing and show the court's reasons. No reasons are required for a default judgment *(Versäumnisurteil)*. Dissenting opinions and the names of the parties are, as a rule, not published except for cases before the federal or state constitutional courts. Decisions are referred to by the date of issue. Only selected judgments are published, and these rarely with the full text.

Settlement

At a given stage during the suit, the court will usually make an attempt to bring about conciliation and settlement. This is generally the rule for lower courts, but often enough the courts of appeal act in the same way. If accepted by the parties, such settlement is enforceable in the same manner as a judgment. A settlement made outside of court is merely a contract between the parties which cannot be enforced except by court action and resulting judgment.
In the case of financial claims, the obligated party may subject itself, without litigation, to execution in a document recorded by a notary.

Costs

German court costs are fixed by statute. The rates are based upon the litigation value. They are quite substantial, particularly for proceedings in the Federal Supreme Court. The losing party has to bear all costs including the statutory fees of the winning party's attorney and necessary expenditures. Fees for witnesses are part of the court costs. Every judgment must contain an adjudication on the allocation of costs among the parties.

Court costs for a law suit must be advanced before the court will act. Therefore, a foreign national, like any German national filing a suit, must make an advance towards the court's costs. Upon the request of the defendant, plaintiffs of foreign nationality and stateless persons without residence in Germany are obliged to post security for the costs of the law suit (court's and defendant's costs) except in some special actions, such as in a special action based upon negotiable instruments or in a cross-action (counter claim).

No such security must be furnished by the foreign plaintiff, however, if, according to the laws in force in the plaintiff's homeland, a German national would not be required to furnish security under identical circumstances (reciprocity).

FOREIGN JUDGMENTS

need not be confirmed by a German court. They are recognized, if final, subject to a number of conditions, mainly reciprocity and proper jurisdiction according to German law and applicable international conventions. If recognized, the foreign judgment has the same effect as a German judgment except for its enforceability. Enforcement of a foreign judgment requires a special decree of a German court. The principle of mutual recognition of judgments is based upon these preconditions. The recognition and execution of judgments of courts of the original six member states of the European Community is regulated in the Convention of 1973.

BANKRUPTCY PROCEEDINGS

apply to all seizable assets belonging to the debtor at the time of the institution of the proceedings, in principle, therefore, also to assets abroad. The effect on the latter is dependent, of course, on the applicable foreign law. Bankruptcy of a German branch of a foreign domiciled enterprise, however, is limited to that branch. The managing directors or liquidators of a corporation must petition the court for the institution of the proceedings in the cases of over-indebtedness or insolvency of the enterprise. Over-indebtedness can be disregarded for such purpose if it is caused by a loan given by a shareholder or any other party and if the lender had agreed to be paid only after all other debts of the company are satisfied. A shareholder loan given in lieu of otherwise needed share capital can be treated as share capital, and if repaid before the undercapitalization or illiquidity of the company is remedied, may even be reclaimed by the company to satisfy creditors. The debtor is not discharged with the termination of the bankruptcy proceedings. He remains liable for unsatisfied debts whether or not such debts were made part of the proceedings. Employees are compensated by the government for privileged salaries and wages which cannot be satisfied because of the insolvency or bankruptcy of their employer. Company pensions are partly secured against insolvency or bankruptcy of the employer by a pension security fund to which all employers have to contribute. Similarly deposits with private banks are to a large extent secured by a deposit protection fund. Bankruptcy may in some cases be avoided by

a general settlement,

a composition of creditors through special court proceedings *(Vergleichsverfahren)* if a proposal is submitted which offers the pro rata cash payment of at least 35 per cent of the debts. The debtor must report to the court also his foreign assets and foreign creditors and debtors. These are included in the proceedings although the recognition abroad of such a German judicial settlement depends on the respective foreign law.

ARBITRATION

The Code of Civil Procedure contains detailed provisions for arbitration, the constitution of the board, procedure, award and its enforcement. Foreign nationals or residents may conclude arbitration agreements according to these provisions. They may also conclude arbitration agreements governed by foreign rules of procedure but intended to be enforced in Germany.

If an arbitration agreement is governed by German procedure, its special rules require attention. Thus the agreement must be explicit with regard to the subject of arbitration; it must be in writing and the instrument may not contain stipulations other than those which have reference to the arbitral proceeding. These formal requirements do not apply if all the contracting parties are merchants within the meaning of the Commercial Code and if the arbitration agreement is a business transcation for both parties; each party may, however, demand that a written instrument be made. If arbitration proceedings are subject to German law each party appoints one arbitrator. If a party fails to do so the arbitrator will be appointed by the court. If the two arbitrators cannot agree on an award the arbitration agreement terminates. It is advisable therefore to provide for one or three arbitrators and for the institution appointing the arbitrators if the parties cannot agree.

In the absence of other provisions of applicable international agreements, a

foreign award

may be declared enforceable by the procedure prescribed for German awards, provided the award is binding according to the governing foreign law. The grounds for which German courts may decline to declare a foreign award enforceable are limited. Foreign arbitral awards may be declared enforceable regardless of reciprocity.

Institutional arbitration

at stock – or commodity exchanges follows the rules of custom and technique of the particular institution. The otherwise applicable rules of law and procedure can be quite different. Whether or not a party is bound by institutional arbitration, especially in international trade, is often a point of controversy. According to the German Stock Exchange Law, agreements to submit to arbitration by stock exchange arbitration boards are binding only if both parties are qualified merchants under the Stock Exchange Law, or if the arbitration agreement was made after the matter in controversy arose. In the field of

international arbitration

the institution and the rules of conciliation and arbitration of the International Chamber of Commerce, Paris, are of major practical importance.

PENAL LAW

no longer applies to offences of a non-criminal nature under a great number of statutory provisions. Instead, fines are levied by administrative agencies, which are subject to judicial review upon motion of the offender. The respective Law on Administrative Offences (*Gesetz über Ordnungswidrigkeiten*) covers numerous minor penal provisions in the fields of fiscal law, trade regulation, antitrust, foreign exchange control, banking, corporations, utilities and traffic violations. Procedure in the case of offences follows the Code of Criminal Procedure. International jurisdiction, i. e. German jurisdiction over foreign domiciled persons or enterprises, is assumed if the respective German substantive law (e. g. tax or cartel law) claims application to such persons or enterprises. Proper service of process on non-resident foreigners in the case of administrative offences is, however, still a somewhat unsolved problem.

V. FOREIGN LAW AND CONFLICT OF LAWS

FOREIGN LAW

may govern business relations in Germany where such law applies in consequence of the German rules of conflict of laws. The introductory statute to the Civil Code contains a few incomplete rules on the choice of law such as to legal capacity, forms of transactions and tort. Implementation of these rules and rules in the many areas of conflict of laws on which the introductory statute is silent (especially contracts, agency, corporations, property) are judge-made law or legal doctrine. Foreign public law (like penal, tax or cartel law) is not applied in principle. Moreover, foreign law is not applied if its application would be contrary to German public policy (ordre public). If the foreign law referred to by the German rules of conflict of laws refers back to German law (renvoi, *Rückverweisung*) or on to the law of a third country (double renvoi, *Weiterverweisung*) such reference is accepted by the German court. Renvoi principles are, however, not followed if the foreign substantive law is to apply pursuant to the parties' intentions. If foreign law is to apply, the German court may request both parties to show its contents but neither party has the burden of proof. For finding the foreign law the court may rely on the parties or make its own investigations. The Federal Republic has ratified the European Convention (of 1968) on Information on Foreign Law. The convention obligates the ratifying countries to give information through the medium of special government agencies to courts of law of the other country in pending cases on their civil and commercial law, the respective laws of procedure and the court systems. The courts are not bound by the contents of the information given. Foreign substantive law – like a fact – is not reviewed by the higher court where the appeal is restricted to points of law.

LEGAL CAPACITY

of natural persons follows the law of nationality and in the case of stateless persons the law of their residence. The capacity of corporations is determined by the law of the actual center of administration, not by the law of incorporation.

THE FORM OF A TRANSACTION

is in principle governed by the law which governs the substance of the transaction, but the observance of the law of the place of transaction suffices. The form for the disposition of title to property as a rule follows the lex situs (lex rei sitae).

ASSIGNMENTS

generally follow the law governing the obligation to assign. The transfer of registered shares of a stock corporation must comply with the law of registry. Assignments of title to shares in a German *GmbH* and resolutions of their shareholders which involve amendments of articles of association, mergers and other structural changes must comply with the essentials of German notarial form. The same applies to the records of shareholders' meetings of German stock corporations. The law governing

CONTRACTUAL RELATIONS

is determined primarily according to the expressed, implied, or presumed intentions of the parties. The presumed intentions are determined pursuant to the "center of gravity" of the contract. If the intentions cannot be ascertained, the law of the place of performance of the individual obligation concerned shall govern by an old rule which in present jurisdiction is considered only if it is a significant indication of the "center of gravity" of the contract. The parties' express or implied stipulation of the applicable law is recognized by the court unless the chosen foreign law has no reasonable relation whatsoever to the case. Such reasonable relation is not necessarily defined by a relation of the facts of the case to a particular country. The parties may validly agree on a "neutral" law, as often practiced, for instance, between a non-German Western firm and an Eastern Bloc trade agency in East-West trade in favor of the law of the Federal Republic of Germany. In view of the uncertainties of the finding of the proper law of contract its stipulation is advisable. The Federal Republic has not ratified the Hague Convention of 1955 on the Law applicable to the International Sale of Goods, nor the Hague Convention of 1956/58 on the Law applicable to the Transfer of Title in the International Sale of Goods. The Hague Convention of 1964 embodying the uniform substantive law of contract on the international sale of goods has been ratified by the Federal Republic. An amending convention regulating the limitation of

25

actions and of periods within which certain notifications of parties to the contract must be made is expected to be ratified. The uniform law applies to private as well as to commercial sales but is of little practical value for the many reservations allowed to the ratifying countries, although it is the result of long extended international comparative law studies and a rare example of integrated Continental civil law and Anglo-American law concepts. A European draft (1972) of a Convention on the Law applicable to Contracts generally and to obligations apart from contract tries to establish much needed firm rules for the applicable law in the wide field of international obligations.

Whatever law may apply to the internal relationship between

principal and agent,

the law applying to the agent's powers towards third parties is determined separately by the law of the state where the agent acts *(Wirkungsstaat)*. If a foreign resident or a foreign enterprise appoints a paying agent or other representative in Germany, the extent of the agent's power is therefore defined by German law. The same principle applies to non-permanent agents, if their authority concerns business matters only. The rights and liabilities incurred by a corporation through the acts of its

corporate officers

are governed by the laws of the state in which the actual center of administration of the corporation is located; even here, however, the local trade is protected: Thus, the president of an American corporation who had signed a guaranty agreement in Berlin was held to have bound the corporation because, under German law, the corporate officers have such authority; the corporation was estopped from showing limitations of the president's power under its charter and bylaws.

PROPERTY

The transfer of title to property is governed by German law under the lex situs when the property in question is situated in

Germany. Contracts concerning the rental or leasing of movable or immovable property are governed by the lex situs, although in this case the applicable law may also be stipulated. Whether the lex situs applies to goods in transit is not established in all cases except that attachment of goods and statutory liens of carriers or repair shops follow the law of the state where such goods happen to be.

Ships are subject to the law of their home ports, aircraft to the law of the country of registration.

Securities

Shares are determined by the law which applies to the corporation, bearer bonds by the law of the place of their issue unless the applicable law has expressly been stipulated differently. With regard to

bills of exchange and checks,

the Geneva Conventions of 1930 and 1931 contain uniform substantive and conflict of law rules which have been transcribed into German national law. The obligation of each party from such instruments must be determined separately. Most European and Latin American states are parties to those conventions, but Great Britain and the United States of America are not members. Protesting of a bill of exchange or a cheque for non-payment by a person authorized to do so under domestic law is recognized without further legalization between the Federal Republic and Denmark, France and Italy.

VI. CONTRACT AND TORT

A CONTRACT

exists under German law when, through an offer and through the acceptance of the offer, the parties agree on the subject matter. Consideration is not a legal requirement for the validity of a contract. A contractual obligation may be entirely one-sided or may be stipulated without any reference to its cause. A contract in favor of a third party by which such party acquires a direct right to make a claim is recognized.

Subject to certain statutory prohibitions and "good morals" *(gute Sitten)*, complete freedom of contract exists. The parties may agree on any matter and in any manner desired. There is no statutory obligation to contract, or not to discriminate in contracts, except for public utilities, public carriers, others in similar or market-dominating positions and for privileges permitted under cartel law. Contracts require no specific

form

unless expressly prescribed by statutory provisions. An oral agreement, therefore, may be as valid and enforceable in court as a written document provided that there is proof of such oral agreement. A written agreement is required for leases of real estate exceeding one year, for acknowledgements of debt or for a guaranty of the obligation of another. Permitted agreements in restraint of trade must be in writing. Written form does not require the witnessing of a signature. A higher degree of formality – recording by a notary qualified pursuant to German law – is required, for example, for the obligation to sell or buy real estate, for certain corporate transactions and the assignment of *GmbH* shares.

Interpretation

of contracts is based upon the expressed or implied true intention of the contracting parties. Good faith, with due regard to common custom, is a rule of interpretation. The actual intention of the parties is to be ascertained from the stipulations employed. There are elaborate provisions in codes and statutes designed to construe party declarations, in case of error, dissent and their consequences, and to supplement points on which the true intention of the parties cannot be ascertained. If a part of the contract is void, the remainder is also void unless it may be assumed that the contract would have been made even without the void part. Because of this uncertainty, a clause is recommended which obligates the parties to make amendments which come as close as possible to any stipulation which might turn out to be void. All of the more common

types of contract

are regulated in some detail in the Civil and Commercial Codes and special statutes – for example sales (now amended for the international sale of goods by the law of the Hague Convention of 1964), loans, leases and service agreements of various types, partnership agreements, corporate agreements, insurance contracts, etc.

The supreme law of contract,

however, remains the expressed or implied intention of the parties at the time when the contract was made. From this, courts have developed a remedy in case of frustration of the originally intended purpose of the contract: if a party can show that the jointly understood essential basis of the contract (*Geschäftsgrundlage*) did not in fact exist, or no longer exists due to intervening circumstances, it may demand an equitable adaptation of the mutual rights and duties to the new situation. This means that the court may rewrite, and in extreme cases rescind the contract. Such a decision is not lightly taken; the doctrine constitutes no general clausula rebus sic stantibus.

Standard Business Conditions

of certain German business branches (e. g. of forwarders and carriers, banks, insurance companies, or commodity trades) and also of individual enterprises on forms for the sale or procurement of goods are very common. Thus in the sale of goods and services the classic contents and legal treatment of contracts and their breach in the codes have become theoretical to some extent. A uniform contract form is widely used for the renting of office and apartment space.

will be recognized only if they are expressly or tacitly accepted by the other party. Even then the courts consider one-sided inequitable terms as contra bonos mores and, therefore, void. Unclear wording is interpreted at the expense of the formulating party. Conflicts between general business conditions of the seller and those of the buyer have been decided against the party having accepted the conditions of the other party without raising objections in due course. The case law has been partly incorporated in the Law on General Business Conditions giving the Chambers of Industry and Commerce – regional public corporations with mandatory membership of all commercial enterprises within the region *(Industrie- und Handelskammer)*, consumer protection associations and certain other institutions the right to intervene against the use of certain conditions considered as inequitable. General conditions may constitute trade usage between merchants in case of doubt the Cambers of Industry and Commerce will be asked by the court to make the necessary findings. Agreements between competitors on uniform business conditions are subject to the cartel law; the cartel authority may also intervene with regard to general business conditions of market-dominating enterprises.

Contractual Liability

A party is fully responsible for breach of contract, i. e. for the intentional or negligent violation of its contractual obligations. Except for failure to pay, breach of contract is predicated upon "fault" in failure to perform.

This extends to action or omission by all persons whom a party employs or uses to discharge its contractual obligations, including employees, agents or any other person so used. Misleading actions or representations made in contract negotiations – culpa in contrahendo – may give a claim for damages to the other party whether a contract was finally concluded or not. Parties are held to owe to each other a measure of trust in their negotiations intended to lead to the conclusion of a contract. This may include the obligation to see to it that the other party is aware of the risks of a contract. Here again the courts tend to protect the weaker against the stronger party wherever the latter abuses its power or superior knowledge.

TORT

is defined in the Civil Code as the intentional or negligent violation – by action or omission to act – of the life, body, health, freedom, property or other right of a person. Among such rights is included the lawful exercising of an existing business (*eingerichteter und ausgeübter Gewerbebetrieb*). Included is also the violation of a statute which is designed to protect another. The term

protective statute (*Schutzgesetz*)

is broadly interpreted. It comprises all laws, statutes, regulations, ordinances and even individual permits issued by proper public authorities which contain such protective clauses. Violation of penal laws, safety regulations in industry and violations of traffic laws are examples.

Liability for Agents

If an officer, employee, servant or agent of an enterprise commits a tort in the execution of his duties or assignment, the enterprise may also be liable. The law makes a distinction here between ordinary employees of an enterprise and the legal representative of a corporation. In the first case, the enterprise has a defense against liability if it can show due diligence in the selection and direction of the employed person and in the procuring – if pertinent – of such person's tools or other equipment. The corporation has no such excuse if the tort was committed by a legal representative in the execution of his proper functions. Such representative of a corporation is a functionary provided for in the corporation's constitution, bylaws or charter or articles of association, known as an "organ" of the corporation, as distinguished from a mere employee. The courts have, however, extended the "organ" theory of the code

31

to include such managing employees who as a result of decentralization have authority to make decisions which would – without such decentralization – be the business of proper organs. The operators of machines or installations, if the latter are the source of

certain typical dangers,

are liable for resulting damages regardless of negligence *(Gefährdungshaftung)* only, if a statute especially so provides. Examples of strict statutory liability of this nature which is limited in principle to the insurable risk include the owner-operator *(Halter)* of an automobile or aircraft, the operator of an atomic energy plant, or a person or enterprise which permits certain defined waste to flow into waterways.
In cases where no privity of contract exists

product liability

has been established by Federal Supreme Court decisions as follows: If injury to a person or damage to property results from the normally intended use of a faulty product, the manufacturer has the burden of proof that he is not responsible for the fault. He is liable for the damage pursuant to the law of tort if he is unable to supply such proof. Contrary to the German and to regulations in other member states the European Commission has in 1976 proposed a directive for the harmonizing of the laws of the member states to the effect that product liability shall exist irrespective of the manufacturer's fault.

VII. AGENTS AND REPRESENTATIVES

German law strictly distinguishes between the external authority of an agent to act *(Vollmacht)* and the internal rights and obligations between principal and agent *(Auftrag)*. *Vollmacht* as an abstract power is separately defined in the Civil Code, while the transaction upon which such power may rest follows the law of contract and most frequently is in the nature

32

of a mandate. Both the power of representation and the underlying mandate or other agreement follow their own rules. Thus, the principal may be bound towards third parties by the statements of the agent, but the agent is liable for damages if he does not respect the internal restrictions of the power of attorney. An agent acting without authority becomes personally liable for the consequences of such acts, unless the principal subsequently ratifies the statements made in his name.

STATUTORY POWER

The scope of a *Vollmacht* is often fixed by statute and cannot be restricted with respect to third parties. Thus a private corporation is bound by the acts of its officers although the authority of such officers may be limited internally. The rationale of this is not an "apparent" authority but the statutory authority of the elected officer as the "organ" of the corporation. It is, therefore, not necessary to show an external situation of "holding out" the authority with the principal's consent.

Authority by Estoppel

In addition to such statutory authority. German courts recognize authority by estoppel *(Duldungs-* or *Anscheinsvollmacht)* and protect the third party in its reliance upon the external fact of such a "holding out".

Undisclosed principal

The German concept of agency is limited to and predicated upon open acts, i. e. disclosed agency. The primary German rule, as laid down in the Civil Code, is that an agent acting in his own name (i. e. without disclosing the fact that he is acting as an agent) does not acquire rights or incur liabilities directly for his principal. In this event the agent only acquires rights as his own and is personally liable. There is no legal relationship between the principal and the other party. The agent, therefore, must make it clear to the other party that he acts not only in the principal's interest but also in the principal's name in order to make the principal the exclusive party.

33

An exception

to the rule that the agency relationship requires an openly declared intention of the agent has been made only in cases where the identity of the party dealing with the business partner is immaterial. This rule has been applied mainly to cash bargains.

One party only –

it is a corollary of this narrow concept that the acts of representation can only bind one party, namely the principal, but never the principal and in addition the agent. The third party has only the principal as a debtor in the case of disclosed agency and only the agent in the case of undisclosed agency, but never both. German law does not permit election between the agent or the principal.

Self-dealing

The Civil Code excludes the authority of an agent to act at the same time for himself and for a principal, or to act for two or more principals in a transaction between them, unless his action is confined to the fulfilment of an existing obligation. As an exception "contracting with one-self" is permissible, provided the authority to do so is specifically granted in the power of attorney by exempting the agent from the respective rule of the Civil Code.

As a rule a power of attorney does not require the form prescribed for the legal transaction to which the authority relates. However, in cases where the form-free granting of the power of attorney would result in the evasion of form requirements applicable to the transaction itself, the power of attorney must be given in the same form as is required for the transaction itself. An example are irrevocable powers of attorney authorizing the sale or purchase of real estate.

The power to act

in the name and on behalf of another – unless already conferred by statute upon persons such as corporate officers – is created through express or implied appointment by the principal. As a rule, no specific form is required for such appointment, but there are exceptions to this. The signature of the principal must be certified by a notary in a number of proceedings, as in all matters involving entries into the Title Register, into the Commercial Register, or in the formation of corporations. Even where no specific form is mandatory it is recommended that foreign enterprises should supply their agents in Germany with at least a written power of attorney – if only to prove and to define the agent's scope of authority. It is further advisable to make the power conform as closely as possible to the forms commonly used in Germany. Sufficient evidence should be contained in the document or attached to it to show that the principal is authorized to grant the respective powers to the agent.

Once conferred,

the power will continue to be valid until its purpose is accomplished or until it is properly revoked and notice thereof is duly given to all parties who may otherwise reasonably rely upon its continuation. If a formal power of attorney was handed to the agent or to a third person, it will only cease to be effective if the document is returned to the principal or declared void by court decision. As a matter of precaution, therefore, the documents should contain a clause binding the holder to return it to the principal upon request. Also, agency powers should – if not for a limited purpose – be granted for a limited time in order to avoid the difficulties which may arise in connection with their revocation. The party dealing with the holder of a power is, however, not protected if he knew or negligently did not know of the expiration or revocation of the power of attorney.
Apart from the definition of the scope of authority of corporate officers, certain generally applicable types of representatives in business enterprises are defined by statute. The most important of these is the so-called

Prokura.

It is granted to managing employees and enables the *Prokurist* to administer the business with a considerable amount of discretion. The *Prokurist* has authority to act for the principal in all matters arising in the course of the business, except for the sale and encumbrance of real estate, unless the latter field is expressly included in the grant. Any restrictions of this power, though binding on the *Prokurist* in his relationship to the enterprise, will not be effective towards third parties, except that a *Prokurist* may be appointed to act jointly with the principal or with another officer of the enterprise. *Prokura* can only be granted by the owner or the legal representative of a commercial enterprise through express appointment and must be entered into the Commercial Register. The *Prokura* is effective with the grant and not only after the act has been registered. The same applies to the authority of the legal representatives of a corporation. The revocation of such authority is similarly effective with the act of revocation but before registration a bona fide third party is protected. The powers of an employee may be limited with respect to third parties in the case of

Handlungsvollmacht

which requires no specific form and is not registered. This power is granted for the special field assigned to the employee. Such power will be assumed where the principal permits the agent-employee to sign business letters or perform other tasks which imply some degree of representation. The designation

Direktor

as widely used in Germany by officers and managing employees of business enterprises is a mere title and has no defined legal meaning, while the appointment of a person as

Generalbevollmächtigter,

i. e. a generally authorized person, confers upon him wide powers to represent an individual, an enterprise or several enterprises. Often enough, even the *Generalbevollmächtigte* is internally restricted to certain business, i.e. beyond this the designation takes the character of a mere title.

The Commercial Code defines and regulates various other types of agency relations such as trade agents, brokers and commission merchants.

THE TRADE AGENT

(Handelsvertreter) is an independent merchant (as distinguished from the dependent employee) who generates business for a principal and, if so authorized, also concludes the contracts for him and in his name. Both parties may request that the agency agreement be in writing. The relationship between the principal and the agent is basically that of a service agreement and the agent's authority follows from the agreement. However, if the agent exceeds his authority the transaction is deemed to have been approved by the principal unless the principal rejects the transaction vis-á-vis the third party immediately after he has learned about it. In any event, the agent is deemed to have been authorized to receive, on behalf of the principal, notice of defective merchandise and similar notices. The agent who has been authorized to conclude contracts in the name of the principal does not have the power to alter contract provisions or to grant an extension of time for payment, nor to accept payments unless such authority has been specifically conferred upon the agent. The agent is entitled to a

commission,

the rate of which may be freely negotiated. The government has not yet made use of the authority under the Commercial Code to establish minimum commissions for agents who act for one principal only. If there is no stipulation between the parties, the agent is entitled to the rate which is customary in the trade. Normally, the commission is earned with respect to all business transactions which have resulted from the agent's activities in some way or other, including follow-up orders from the customer. If the agent has been assigned a specific territory or a specific group of customers, he is entitled to the commission even if he has not generated or concluded the transaction. The agent also earns a commission for transactions which are concluded within a reasonable time after the termination of the agency agreement if he has generated or initiated or substantially prepared the transaction. An additional commission is earned for collections. The parties may, however, agree on more limited provisions or even exempt certain transactions from commissions – for example, direct sales by the principal. The agent also earns a special commission if he assumes the liability for the performance of the customer in individual transactions *(Delcredere)*. This rule does not apply if either the principal or customer maintains his business establishment or domicile outside of Germany.

Termination

If the agency agreement is entered into for an indefinite period of time it may be terminated only to the end of a calendar quarter. During the first three years, prior notice must be six weeks and thereafter three months. The notice period may be shortened by agreement to one month before the end of a calendar month, however, only during the first three years. Any agreed notice period must be the same for both parties. An agreement with the agent to refrain from competition after termination of the agreement may not extend to more than two years after the effective date of termination and must provide for an adequate compensation. The agent may have a claim to special

compensation

after termination of the agency agreement. This claim *(Ausgleichsanspruch)* is intended as a compensation for the principal's continuing benefit from business and goodwill created through the agent's activities. The compensation must appear equitable under the circumstances. The amount of compensation is at the most a one-year commission computed on the basis of the average commissions during the five years prior to termination, or such shorter period as may have been the case. The compensation claim cannot be excluded or waived in advance. There is no such claim if the termination by the principal is based on cause for which the agent is at fault or if the agent himself terminates, unless the principal has given cause or if such termination is made for the reasons of the age or illness of the agent. The claim to compensation as well as some of the other mandatory provisions of the trade agency law, may also be raised by a

DISTRIBUTOR

who sells in his own name and for his own account (*Eigenhändler*), provided the distributor as well as an authorized dealer (*Vertragshändler*), was integrated into the marketing organization of the principal in a manner comparable to that of a trade agent and the provisions of the distribution agreement require the distributor to disclose his customer relationships to the manufacturer in such a manner as to enable the latter to use them to his advantage after termination of the agreement. Even then, the distributor is not entitled to the compensation if his former customers continue to deal with the manufacturer simply because of the latter's widely recognized trademark, an effect described by the Federal Supreme Court as the "sucking" effect of the manufacturer's brand upon the consumer public. Principals may be able to avoid the liability to compensate their ex-agents (and "agent"-distributors) by subjecting the agreement to less protective

foreign law

only if the parties' bona fide relations warrant this. If both principal and agent maintain a business establishment or a domicile in Germany and if the agency activities concern Germany, the agreement on non-German law would probably be held invalid as an attempted evasion of German law. However, if the principal is a non-resident, German law may be avoided by subjecting the agreement to the foreign law of the principal. If the agent maintains no business establishment in

Germany but rather carries out his activities in Germany from a foreign establishment, the agreement may also be made subject to the foreign law. Conversely, a German principal may subject the agreement with an agent abroad to the foreign law. Even if German law applies to an agency abroad, the parties are free to deviate in every respect from the restrictions of German law.

VIII. SECURED TRANSACTIONS

THE GERMAN *Bürgschaft*

is normally what is generally referred to in American terminology as a guaranty. Claims against the promisor *(Bürge)* exist only to the extent that a claim can be made against the primary debtor and the *Bürge* is obligated to pay only after default of the primary debtor. If a creditor is to have the right upon default to proceed against the *Bürge* unconditionally, i. e. immediately, without first exhausting his remedies against the primary debtor, the most common type of *Bürgschaft*, the so-called *selbstschuldnerische Bürgschaft*, is created. Unless a stipulation is made to the contrary, the *Bürgschaft* of a merchant is ipso jure *selbstschuldnerisch*. A *Bürge* has a statutory right of recourse against the primary debtor for the entire amount of the debt which has been discharged.

THE GERMAN *Garantie*

represents an obligation in money which is assumed for a non-monetary performance or a financial obligation owed by another person. In practice, the *Garantie* is more used to guarantee financial obligations, especially in international trade, in connection with *Deutsche Mark* bond issues and generally with loans. In all such cases the promisor in a *Garantie* is an insurer of a certain success or of the existence and payment of a debt. In the case a *Garantie* is given by a corporate subsidiary to secure the debt of an affiliated company, one should be aware of the statutory prohibition of any repayment of the share capital of the guaranteeing corporation.

THE GERMAN *Patronatserklärung,*

is much used for the securing by a corporation of debts of a subsidiary or of an otherwise affiliated enterprise. It constitutes a "comfort letter". Its value greatly varies depending on the scope of the commitment.

THE GERMAN *Pfandrecht,*

a pledge, may be created in respect of chattels or intangibles, e. g. receivables or other claims, securities, *GmbH* shares etc. The form required is the same as applies to a title transfer of the pledged item. Thus, a pledge of tangibles involves as a necessary element the transfer of possession (directly or in charge of another person) of the pledged property from the pledgor to the pledgee. Consequently, the German chattel mortgage in the form of a pledge is lost if the pledgee permits the re-possession of the pledged property by the pledgor. However, there is no necessity nor possibility for the recording of the transaction to give actual or constructive notice to third parties; possession constitutes constructive notice. Only if the property is kept by another person such other person must be notified, as for example, a bank which is holding a security on deposit on behalf of the pledgor.

After the pledge has matured the sale of the pledged item by the pledgee may take place only after notice is given to the pledgor. Pledged items which have a definite market value or a value quoted on stock- or commodity exchanges may be sold informally; other items must be sold at public auction unless a private sale has been agreed upon subsequent to the maturing of the pledge. An agreement that the pledgee shall have title to the pledged asset entered into before the maturity of the pledge is void. A third party having an interest in the pledged item may intervene, and may redeem the item by satisfying the pledgee's claim.

The pledge cannot be transferred without the transfer of the underlying claim. The pledge expires if the claim is satisfied.

41

SECURITY INTERESTS IN CHATTELS AND INTANGIBLES

Briefly and simply stated, the security attained in the United States through conditional sales, chattel mortgages and assignment of accounts and contract claims corresponds to some extent to the German *Eigentumsvorbehalt, Sicherungsübereignung* and *Sicherungsabtretung*. These German forms of security interests were developed to provide for a simpler realization of security interests and for greater freedom of contract than are available in connection with the *Pfandrecht*. The *Eigentumsvorbehalt* resembles the conditional sales contract, the *Sicherungsübereignung* the chattel mortgage and trust receipt, and the *Sicherungsabtretung* the assignment of acounts receivable and contract claims, although the legal structure and the techniques of these legal devices in the two countries have little in common.

There is

no registration system

nor the requirement of possession for so charging chattels or intangibles. Security interests often attach as the result of their inclusion in the standard general terms and conditions of a transaction. The debtor is presumed to have accepted such terms and conditions and has validly entered into a security agreement by not expressly refuting the terms and conditions read or un-read by him if he had reasonable opportunity to learn of the terms and conditions at the time of concluding the contract. The fairness of such terms and conditions is still subject to strict judicial review. Security interests are widely used and are effective against third party creditors even without their knowledge. As a result, in bankruptcy, often enough if not mostly the unsecured creditors lose out and demands for reforming this situation are pressing.

Eigentumsvorbehalt

is characterized as a device by which immediate possession of the goods is given to the purchaser, and the title in the goods is retained by the seller. The title passes to the purchaser upon full

42

payment of the agreed price. Instalment sales are a major field for this kind of security and subject to special statutory regulation in many respects. While the *Eigentumsvorbehalt* is the typical purchase money security interest, i. e., granted by the buyer when the seller extends credit for the goods purchased, the

Sicherungsübereignung

is the grant by the debtor to secure a separate liability in goods already owned (or expected to be owned by the mere possessor). The *Sicherungsübereignung* is created when the parties reach an agreement to transfer title of a chattel as collateral. The agreement must contain an express understanding that the debtor remains in possession as custodian for the creditor. In case of non-payment, the creditor retains full title and can request the transfer of possession. After obtaining actual possession, the secured party can seek satisfaction out of the goods in a commercially reasonable manner. In case of payment, full title automatically reverts to the debtor, if so agreed.

Fixtures *(wesentliche Bestandteile)*

in German law are component parts which cannot be separated from one another without destroying or essentially changing the one or the other. The individual component parts cannot be the object of separate security interests. A security interest in the principal object extends to all component parts of that object. Component parts which are firmly affixed to realty become part of realty and cannot be part also of separate security interest transactions. Fixtures should not be confused with

accessories *(Zubehör)*

– i. e., movables intended to serve the economic purpose of the principal object without being component parts of it; these must expressly be stated if the security interest in the principal object shall include them.

Accessories and components are subject to a mortgage and also to a statutory lien of the landlord which rank prior to a *Sicherungsübereignung* if created prior to the latter. Particular care is required when goods are

processed

and lose their identy. *Eigentumsvorbehalt* or *Sicherungsübereignung* do not necessarily extend to the new product and there are limitations as to special stipulations upon which the parties can agree. Title reservation may be upheld for the supplier of the original product when it is agreed *(Verarbeitungsklausel)* that the processor stands in the shoes of the supplier, acting as the fabricator *(Hersteller)* on his behalf. There are important

amending clauses

applying to *Eigentumsvorbehalt* or *Sicherungsübereignung*. One is a *Verlängerungsklausel* which can be characterized as a device whereby all accounts receivable arising out of the sale of the goods charged are automatically assigned to the seller. If title shall remain charged until all outstanding accounts arising out of a business relationship are satisfied, such clause is called *Kontokorrentvorbehalt*. In the same way the circle of creditors can be extended to secure accounts payable to related or associated companies of the seller: *Konzernvorbehalt*.
Assignment of accounts receivable

Sicherungsabtretung

is perfected by assignment, without any communication to the debtor; but the debtor may make payment to the assignor in fulfilment of his obligation, unless he has knowledge of the assignment. The assignee stands in the shoes of the assignor and is subject to all defenses available against the latter. Also future receivables may be assigned if they are distinctly definable, and other claims which by their nature are assignable. Global assignments of all or most future claims against all or most future debtors to serve as collateral for an open account between a seller and a buyer or a bank and a customer –

Globalzession –

are often held to be invalid for endangering the other creditors of the business. Otherwise the conflict which arises between the bank, giving loans (secured by *Globalzession*), and the supplier, giving credit for goods delivered (secured by way of *verlängerter Eigentumsvorbehalt*) has been decided, as a rule, in favor of the prior transaction.
The requirement of

identification

must be complied with in the case of *Eigentumsvorbehalt* and of *Sicherungsübereignung*, particularly in the case of a *Verlängerungsklausel*, as well as in the case of a *Sicherungsabtretung*, especially in the event of the assignment of future receivables. The requirement pertains to the description of the security as well as to the claim to be secured. In the case of *Sicherungsübereignung*, mere words in the security agreement do not suffice. Identification of the items charged is determined by outward appearances, for example, by separate storage or by marking.
Acquisition of title to or of security interests in tangibles by a

bona fide third party

destroys or gives priority over any prior security interests in tangible property if the third party is unaware of the interest at the time he obtains physical possession of the object secured. The acquisition of unencumbered title by good faith is limited to chattels and does not extend to assignment of intangibles, commercial or non-commercial. On the other hand, it is not limited to a buyer in the ordinary course of business. Thus the giving of consideration or the entering of a commercial transaction are not necessary elements for obtaining full title on behalf of a bona fide third party. There is no following of the trust property in German law. The third party acting in good faith acquires full title. The seller is liable for damages for conversion and is also subject to criminal penalty.

Since the German law on secured transactions is to a remarkable extent based on hidden priorities – on a first come, first served basis – checks and balances against an

overkill

by the first security taker had to be created which prevent the giving of collateral to others in the future. Security interests may not exceed the secured claim by more than an adequate margin. In particular, if the debtor loses his economic independence entirely by signing away all future interests through all-inclusive afteracquired property- and proceeds clauses, a body of law has been developed pursuant to which oppressive security agreements (so-called *Knebelungsverträge*) are inequitable and therefore invalid. In point is in particular the *Globalzession*. In the same vein, collateral agreements are also invalid if the agreement includes the consequence to defraud present or future creditors of the purchaser, for example if a merchant buys generally by *Eigentumsvorbehalt* with *Verlängerungsklausel* and assigns his future receivables, or generally if the creditor leaves a shell of substance with the debtor in a manner which deceives other creditors about the debtor's credit capacity. The so secured creditor may be liable for damages to other creditors, for instance if his actions have prevented a timely institution of bankruptcy proceedings of the debtor. German law has no statutory equivalent to the American

Bulk Sales Act.

There is, however, a statutory liability on the part of the transferee, to the extent of the transferred assets, for all debts of the transferor when anybody in the course of business or otherwise, assigns all or substantially all of his assets to a third party. For a few specific types of chattels, German statutory laws have established special registers for perfecting security interests, such as for ships and airplanes,

where a registration is possible under special statutes. The protection is absolute and far-reaching. Unrecorded security transactions are null and void, and the recorded creditor can obtain satisfaction, irrespective of insolvency, bankruptcy, or receivership and irrespective of any lack of knowledge of other creditors or third parties.

SECURITY INTERESTS IN REALTY,

in real estate or land, include the buildings and extend to both, components and accessories of land and buildings. Security interests may be granted also for rights in part in realty such as in apartment ownerships.

Security interests in realty must be entered into the Title Register and their priorities are determined by their filing dates. Two principal categories of non-possessory security interests in land are available – the mortgage *(Hypothek)* and the land charge *(Grundschuld)*. The former is legally accessory to, and dependent upon an underlying personal obligation owed to the mortgagee; the latter, as a matter of law, constitutes a monetary obligation of the land as such, irrespective of the existence of the liability of a personal debtor. An owner may create a land charge for himself on his own property *(Eigentümergrundschuld)*. In this way an owner may save a particular position in the hierarchy of encumbrances for subsequent utilization e. g. for the purpose of assignment. A third party land charge or a mortgage may subsequently become transformed into an owner land charge und thus prevent the moving up of subordinate encumbrances. By an amendment of the statute, however, the holder of a security which was applied for registration after January 1, 1978, may demand the cancellation of the otherwise resulting land charge of the owner. Unless the parties agree otherwise, the creation of a mortgage or land charge is accompanied by the execution and delivery to the creditor of a

certificate evidencing

the mortgage or land charge (*Hypothekenbrief* or *Grundschuldbrief*). The mortgage or land charge certificate is a non-negotiable instrument. The transfer of the claim protected by the security interest, and of the security interest itself, is accomplished by a written assignment and delivery of the certificate. The transferee is entitled to the same position as if the transfer were registered. The debtor cannot be released from his obligation unless he pays the holder of the certificate. Mortgage certificates are not traded as investment paper but

mortgage bonds

(*Pfandbriefe*), issued by mortgage banks (*Hypothekenbanken*) which are based on first priority mortgages are very popular securities.

IX. ENTERPRISE FORMS AND BUSINESS PERMITS

German law provides for a great variety of

ENTERPRISE FORMS:

the individual merchant or single trader, several forms of partnerships and corporations, mining corporations, co-operatives and others. State-owned industry and major utilities operate in the form of private corporations. Public corporations or public institutions (*öffentliche Anstalten*) participate in business, in particular in the fields of private banking and private insurance. Private trusts are not suitable as an enterprise form.

The "association for a joint purpose" the general German legal concept of "*Gesellschaft*" covers practically all associations of civil and of commercial law; in particular the partnerships, the corporations (or companies) and the mixed enterprise forms as shown in the chart and explained in detail in this chapter.

48

The German Concept of "Gesellschaft" and respective Enterprise Forms*)

Gesellschaft
association for a joint purpose

Personalgesellschaft
partnership

Kapitalgesellschaft
corporation

Bürgerliche Gesellschaft
civil law partnership
(used also for joint business
holdings and consortia)

Handelsgesellschaft
commercial law
partnership

Offene Handelsgesellschaft (OHG)
general partnership

all partners
with unlimited liability

Personalistische KG
partnership with managing
individuals

Kommanditgesellschaft (KG)
limited partnership
managing partners with
unlimited, others with
limited liability

Kapitalistische KG
partnership with
managing corporation

GmbH (or AG) & Co KG
one or more corporations are
the sole managing partners,
all with "unlimited" liability
(in the classic form partners
share equally in *GmbH* (or *AG*)
capital and in *KG* capital)

Aktiengesellschaft (AG)
stock corporation

Bergrechtliche Gewerkschaft
mining corporation

Kommanditgesellschaft auf Aktien (KGaA)
stock corporation with unlimited
liability of managing partners

Gesellschaft mit beschränkter Haftung (GmbH)
company with limited liability

*) Not included: Public corporations and institutions,
foundations of private or public law, mutual
insurance- and building loan associations,
cooperative business societies and silent partnerships.

Personal Liability

Unlimited liability governs the business conducted in form of single proprietorship *(Einzelkaufmann)*. Two standard forms of personal partnership exist: The general partnership *(Offene Handelsgesellschaft: OHG)* and the limited partnership *(Kommanditgesellschaft: KG)*. In the *OHG* all partners are personally liable without limitation. In the *KG* one or more active general partners are liable without limitation *(Komplementär)* while one or more limited partners are liable only to the amount of their fixed contribution to the partnership *(Kommanditist)*. It is quite common and legal in *KG* agreements to give a *Kommanditist* broad rights of control over the seemingly more important figure of the *Komplementär*, especially where the contribution of the *Kommanditist* or of the party represented by him is substantial. The courts have permitted corporations to be partners of an *OHG* and of a *KG*. A general corporate partner in the *OHG* or *KG* remains liable only pursuant to corporation law, i. e. without committing its shareholders beyond their share investment.

Partnership Status

All forms of partnership use a registered name under which they carry on their business, have a domicile, may acquire, hold and dispose of property, may sue and may be sued. Each partner becomes the owner of an undivided share of the entire assets of the partnership. The partnership agreement is not public nor subject to a prescribed form – it is usually in writing. The principle of freedom of contract prevails. The silent partnership *(stille Gesellschaft)* is only internally a partnership under German law; externally the silent partner is rather a special type of creditor. His contribution becomes part of the active partner's business assets and the active partner or partnership alone is responsible for the business in which the silent partner invests. The simple civil law association *(BGB Gesellschaft)* is also used for business purposes such as the pooling of joint interests in lasting or short-term ventures; every partner of such association is personally liable as in an *OHG* but

50

the civil law association cannot operate under a registered firm name. For the carrying out of joint construction projects by several enterprises, the *BGB Gesellschaft*, adapted to such purpose internally and externally, is called *Arbeitsgemeinschaft: ARGE*; for other purposes the name *Konsortium* is used, especially by banks for joint credit operations or for bond issues.

Corporations

Apart from mining corporations, there are two common forms of private law corporations, the Stock Corporation *(Aktien-gesellschaft: AG)* and a corporation of a more personal character, the Company with Limited Liability *(Gesellschaft mit be-schränkter Haftung: GmbH)*.

Mixed Enterprise Forms

In addition to the practice that corporations may be simply partners in personal companies, there are special combinations between corporate and personal partnership forms. A combination much in use is a *Kommanditgesellschaft* in which there is only one general partner, a corporation, in most cases a *Gesellschaft mit beschränkter Haftung*. In the classic form of this combination each limited partner of this *GmbH & Co KG* holds a share in the *GmbH* in proportion to his holding in the *KG*. The *GmbH's* share capital, i. e. the capital of the only generally liable partner, the *GmbH*, often enough does not exceed the statutory minimum share capital for a *GmbH*. The *GmbH & Co KG* is recognized under commercial law as well as under tax law as a partnership. For the application of the 1976 Co-determination Law, pursuant to which a corporation having 2000 or more employees must have a co-determined supervisory board, the employees of the *KG* are counted as employees of the corporate general partner if the majority by capital of the limited partners holds the majority of the *GmbH*.

Another combination of corporate and personal liability is the corporation with general partner(s), *Kommanditgesellschaft auf Aktien: KGaA*, a form adapted from the French Code de

Commerce and expressly regulated by the Stock Corporation Law. This is a corporation with regular shareholders and with one or more personally liable natural persons who constitute the legal representatives and managing directors of the *KGaA*. These persons may also hold shares or make other capital contributions to the corporation. This special enterprise form is not much in use, however.

Changes of enterprise form, mergers and consolidations

are widely possible without requiring that the concerned enterprises first go into liquidation, and since 1969 without inequitable tax consequences which were hitherto prohibitive in many cases.

Corporate forms are interchangeable,

for example, an *AG* may be converted into a *GmbH* or vice versa. A general or limited partnership or a single business may simply be converted into a new, or merge into an existing corporation, and a corporation may change into a personal partnership or single business. An *AG* may be merged with another *AG* or several *AGs* may be merged into a new *AG* formed for the purpose of consolidation. A *GmbH* may be merged with an *AG*. But a *GmbH* may, technically speaking, not be merged with another *GmbH*, however there are solutions which assure the same result.

The procedures

for changes of enterprise form and for merger or consolidation are simple. Partnership decisions for such purposes must be unanimous provided the partnership agreement does not determine otherwise.

Corporate decisions require, in most cases, the consent of only 3/4 of the votes represented in a properly convened shareholders' meeting. However, for converting an *AG* into a *GmbH*, all *AG* shareholders must agree, or if there are less than 50 shareholders 9/10 of the share capital must so agree. In addition the corporation must offer to buy out any objecting shareholders.

BUSINESS PERMITS

are not required for most commercial undertakings in Germany. But the enterprise or its management must show proper qualification and obtain a permit for some business activities such as banking, insurance or the retail trades. Foreign corporations still must be admitted to operate a branch in Germany unless they qualify as nationals within the European Economic Community – EEC. All new enterprises must report to the local trade tax authority at the beginning of business. Where permits or admissions are required they must be granted by the respective authorities if the proper qualifications and identities are shown. They must in principle not be refused for a lack of need. Within certain rules

all forms of commercial activity

are open also to the foreigner – companies, individual merchants, business partners, shareholders, members of a board. Managers or employees of a German enterprise or of a German branch of a foreign enterprise may all be foreign nationals and residence in Germany for business owners or executives is a matter of practicality rather than of law with some exceptions.

THE CHOICE

of a foreign enterprise wishing to operate in Germany is usually between a branch office, a subsidiary or a joint venture with another enterprise. The possibility of a branch of the foreign enterprise is seldom chosen. For the joint venture the corporate form is generally preferred. The reasons are in the first place tax considerations.

The branch operation or the ownership of an unincorporated business or participation in a general or limited partnership as a rule commit the foreign owner or partner to more German taxes than the operation through a German corporation. A branch operation is therefore chosen for other reasons, for instance by banks which, for reasons of prestige, want to commit the total resources of the foreign bank, or generally, if losses are to be anticipated for years to come if they can be set-off against the profits of the foreign parent abroad. A reason to prefer the subsidiary corporation could be the limited liability of the shareholders which applies also to the sole shareholder unless the sole owner has represented his liability over and beyond the corporation's liability, or under special circumstances may be found guilty of an abuse. This refusal to pierce the corporate veil has only recently been reconfirmed by the Federal Supreme Court for the somewhat extreme case of an undercapitalized and parent-managed subsidiary. Between the two common types of corporation, *AG* and *GmbH,* the latter is preferable wherever subscription to capital by the public is not needed or wherever the right of the shareholders to take a direct influence upon the actions or measures of the management of the subsidiary corporation shall be established, a special possibility under the *GmbH* Law. In many respects, the

GmbH is the ideal form

for the subsidiary or for the joint venture of partners who depend on their own means and have an operating – or major investment interest – in short for the closed corporation. A good many German and foreign-held enterprises of major importance are *GmbHs*.

X. GMBH AND AG, ENTERPRISE COMBINATIONS, "LARGE" ENTERPRISES

THE *GmbH*

is based upon the agreement of two or more founding partners in a document known as the articles of association of the *GmbH* *(Gesellschaftsvertrag* or *Satzung)*, which must be recorded by a notary. The articles of association represent in one integrated document the incorporation data and the bylaws. The *GmbH* comes into legal existence with a second step which is the entering of the required data into the Commercial Register. Persons acting on behalf of a *GmbH* before such registration are personally liable. The formation of the *GmbH* by proxy is possible. It is permissible for a shareholder to take a share in trust for another shareholder or other person and to agree to the subsequent transfer of the share to such other shareholder or person. A necessary minimum of the articles of association is regulated by statute. Although a good many of the statutory provisions can be amended by agreement , if no such changes are intended – all that is needed to establish the *GmbH* is agreement on the name, the domicile, the intended purpose of business, the amount of capital with the amounts of contribution to it by each shareholder, the person of the managing director and – as a practical matter – an indication of the applicable fiscal year.

The name of the *GmbH*

must contain the words *Gesellschaft mit beschränkter Haftung* (according to a long awaited recent Supreme Court decision the abbreviation *"GmbH"* suffices) and (unless the *GmbH* continues the name of an acquired business) must either consist of the name of at least one shareholder or else indicate the *GmbH's* business. The use of the name of a foreign (company) shareholder may be objected to if such name would not be permissible under German law. A combination of a share-holder's name and the business purpose is permissible. The chosen name must not conflict with already existing business names in the district. The court in registering the *GmbH* shall consult the local Chamber of Industry and Commerce on the chosen name.

The domicile of the *GmbH*

must be within Germany and need not, except for tax purposes, be the actual seat of administration. The statement of the *GmbH's*

business purpose

is a brief listing of its main objectives. The case by case enumeration of detailed business activity or of legal acts the *GmbH* may perform is unnecessary. There is no ultra vires doctrine for corporations of private law. The doctrine applies, however, to officers of public corporations. The *GmbH* through its legal representatives may do all legal acts a natural person is capable of doing in business.

The share capital

must be stated in *Deutsche Mark,* although it may, in whole or in part, be contributed in kind. Contributions in kind must be clearly defined in the articles. The registering court may and more and more as a matter of practice does examine the value of such contributions, although it is not required to do so. The minimum capital is *DM 20,000.–* and the minimum single share is *DM 500.–*. The shares may have different nominal amounts but must be divisible by 100. Upon formation of a *GmbH,* contributions in kind must be fully paid, but only 25 per cent of the value of each share for contributions in cash need be paid in at this time. There are no share assessments unless agreed to in the articles. The shareholders are responsible in proportion to their holdings for the outstanding cash contributions of other shareholders which cannot be collected.

The capital is not split into equally denominated shares. It is not permissible to divide a share – except for the sale or inheritance of a part share. Such division requires the corporation's consent. The shares represent an undivided portion of the *GmbH's* assets.

56

Each share is denominated pursuant to the contribution of its first holder. Thus, for example, a *GmbH* might have only two shares, one of *DM 19,000.–* and the other of *DM 1,000.–*. Certificates are optional but uncommon. They are not negotiable but the articles may provide for their transfer in case of assignment. Restraints on alienation of a share may be liberally agreed to in the articles. A share is transferred or pledged by a notarial record pursuant to German form. The assignment or pledging of shares is often made dependent upon the consent of a simple or specified majority of the shareholders' meeting. Rights of first refusal in the case of a sale of a share must be recorded in notarial form, and to be effective against third parties, must be incorporated into the articles of association.

Amendments of the articles of association

require 75 per cent of the votes, the articles may provide for stricter requirements. The resolution must be recorded by a notary and filed with the Commercial Register to become effective. While there is no requirement where shareholders' meetings must be held, this type of meeting must take place where a notary is able to act who has qualified in a manner similar to a German notary. Representation by proxy is permitted. Resolutions of the shareholders other than those involving amendments of the articles need not be notarized. They may be made orally or in writing without a meeting if all shareholders agree to such procedure. The articles may stipulate

special shareholder rights

and eliminate the statutory provisions prohibiting shareholders from voting in matters which concern transactions between the *GmbH* and the shareholder himself. The shareholder has a direct statutory right to the profits shown in the *GmbH's* annual financial statement in proportion to his shareholding. This provision is often replaced in the articles by the right of the annual shareholders' meeting to decide by a simple or specified majority upon the extent to which such profit shall be distributed or applied to reserves. In addition to special minority rights which may be set forth in the articles, the minority is granted a statutory right to obtain information, to demand a shareholders' meeting, and to cause the meeting to decide on motions made by the minority. The courts give protection against a misuse of majority power or objectives which are outside of the *GmbH's* purpose.

The *GmbH* is legally represented and operated by one or more executives, i. e.

managing directors *(Geschäftsführer)*.

The authority of the *Geschäftsführer* is a statutory authority which is unlimited with respect to third parties. This authority cannot be restricted except by granting two or more *Geschäftsführer* collective authority. The *Geschäftsführer* may be directed in his management actions or measures by the shareholders or be bound internally to obtain the prior approval from the shareholders or other authority for certain types of transactions. Unless the articles of association expressly provide for an exemption from the prohibition of self-dealing the *Geschäftsführer* has no authority to contract between himself and the *GmbH*, unless he is the sole shareholder and the sole *Geschäftsführer* at the same time. The Law permits administrative, consulting or supervisory

boards of directors.

The German institution of a two-tier board system: apart from the (board of) management a non-executive supervisory board *(Aufsichtsrat)*, is mandatory for the *GmbH* if the regular number of employees exceeds 500 and, irrespective of this condition, for capital investment companies *(Kapitalanlagegesellschaften)*. In the first case one-third of the *Aufsichtsrat* members are elected by the employees. Under the Co-determination Law 1976 (which takes effect at the latest in 1978) the "large" *GmbH* (over 2000 employees) must have a supervisory board composed of an equal number of shareholder-elected and employee-elected members (including the special representation of managing employees – *leitende Angestellte*); the chairman (normally elected from the shareholder representatives) has a casting vote in case of a tie; the managing directors are appointed not by the shareholders but – as in the *AG* – by the supervisory board; one of the managing directors shall be primarily responsible for personnel matters.

Financial statements and audits

The Law does not require great detail for the accounting and financial statements of a *GmbH*. A more precise directive has been proposed by the European Commission for all types of corporations. The appointment of independent auditors to examine the *GmbH's* annual financial statements or the publication of such information is not necessary. The statements do not have to be filed with any court or administrative authority. Exceptions apply to banks. Other exceptions apply to certain *GmbHs* as regulated for a *GmbH* controlling a combine, *Konzern*, in the Stock Corporation Law, and in the *Publizitätsgesetz* (Disclosure Law) for *GmbHs* to which at least two of the following criteria apply: a balance sheet total over DM 125 million, sales over DM 250 million, over 5000 employees.

Legislative intentions

A very elaborate bill for a new *GmbH* Law by the Ministry of Justice which was intended to bring the *GmbH* too close to the regulations which apply to the *AG*, has been abandoned presently for a less ambitious bill which is to provide for some amendments, mainly for a better protection of creditors.

The EEC Council of Ministers is expected to issue a directive which will compel *GmbHs* to render account like a stock corporation; consolidated accounts will have to be rendered not only by the ultimate parent company but also by every group company with respect to its subsidiaries and affiliates – so-called Christmas tree principle.

The *Aktiengesellschaft*

also comes into existence by the court's registration of its data. No governmental certificate or permit is needed for its formation nor for the issuance of shares. At least five

founders

are necessary who subscribe to the shares in a notarial record. In such record, the founders also agree to the articles of association *(Satzung)* representing in one integrated document the incorporation data and the bylaws. The articles of association are prescribed in great detail by the Law; a deviation from these provisions is possible only to the limited extent expressly permitted by the Law. The founders appoint the first supervisory board *(Aufsichtsrat)* which appoints the board of management *(Vorstand)*. The founders must render a report on the formation. Both boards must examine the steps of the formation and, in some cases, auditors must make an examination, if, for example, there are contributions in kind for shares or if a founder is a member of one of the boards of the *AG*. Contributions and also the intended acquisition of assets by the *AG* must be stated in the articles. Contracts for certain major acquisitions within the first two years of the existence of the *AG* are subject to special formalities. The minimum

share capital

is DM 100,000.– at least 25 per cent of which must be paid in on each share. Any premium or a contribution in kind must be fully paid in. Under German practice, shares are mostly

bearer shares,

however, partially paid shares and interim certificates must be nominative. Shares must be stated in a nominal *DM* amount, as a minimum with *DM 50.–*. The splitting of shares is permitted only within certain limits. Shares without par value cannot be created. Shares are negotiable securities. The transfer of bearer shares requires no special form. Agreements on restraints on alienation are freely permissible. Stock exchange prices are quoted now throughout as a price per share. The purchase and sale of shares by the individual investor is, as a rule, effected through banks. The shares are normally left in bank custody, and the bank collects the dividends for the shareholder and as a rule acts as his proxy in shareholders' meetings.

The exercising of such voting rights by banks and other professional associations or persons is regulated in the Law. In the

two – tier board system

of the *AG*, the supervisory board and the board of management are distinctly separate. Membership of one and the same person in both boards or a mixed board of directors consisting of managerial and supervisory or advisory members is not possible. A member of the supervisory board may be delegated to the management board for a predetermined limited time, during which such member cannot exercise his functions as a member of the supervisory board. The main functions of the supervisory board are the appointment and removal of the management board members, the final decision – as a rule – on the *AG*'s annual financial statements, the supervision of the management, and – if reserved – the approval, internally, of certain transactions or measures of the management. As a rule, the chairman of the supervisory board presides at the shareholders' meeting. The supervisory board is mandatory for the *AG* and *KGaA*. Except for corporations of the mining and of the iron and steel producing industries, one-third of the members are elected by the employees, and two-thirds by the shareholders' meeting. All members have the same rights. There is no cumulative voting. As in the "large" *GmbH* also the "large" *AG* (over 2000 employees) will now have a supervisory board of equal numbers of shareholder-elected and employee-elected members (including the representation of the managing employees) with a casting vote in case of a tie, of the chairman (normally a representative of the shareholders). With regard to the management,

German practice prefers several members, including a chairman or speaker, who possess collective authority for the *AG's* representation in and out of court, normally by two members jointly. One member of the board of management of the "large" *AG* must be responsible mainly for personnel matters. No member or members of a management board can be granted the right to decide against the board's majority when a conflict of opinion exists but a veto-right may be granted to the chairman. No member may be appointed for a term exceeding five years. Reappointment is permissible. No member may be removed except for cause, however, lack of confidence of the majority of the shareholders may constitute cause.

Shareholder rights

are exercised in shareholders' meetings. As in the *GmbH*, amendments of the articles generally require 75 per cent of the votes represented in a properly convened shareholders' meeting. This applies also to some special decisions such as the issuing of convertible bonds and major structural changes of the enterprise. The meetings must be recorded by a notary. Each shareholder has a right to information. The competent body to give the information is the board of management. Information may only be refused if the answer would cause the *AG* or a connected enterprise a not inconsiderable disadvantage. Minority rights are based upon a certain percentage of the share capital or in some cases upon the holding of a certain aggregate nominal amount of the share capital. Some such rights are exercised by a simple request, others require a court order or litigation. Elections to the supervisory board require the simple majority of the votes cast. The minority has no statutory right to be represented on the board. The articles may provide differently, however. They may also provide for the simple delegation of a person to the board by a certain shareholder or the holder of certain shares, provided the aggregate of such delegated members does not exceed one-third of the members to be appointed by the shareholders. The shareholders have pre-emptive rights in capital increases although these can be excluded by a resolution requiring the consent of 75 per cent of the share capital represented in the meeting. The articles may provide for additional conditions. The dealing with insider problems is the subject of a voluntary regulation for stock corporation insiders promoted by the banks and the stock exchanges.

Annual accounting and reporting

to the shareholders is regulated in the Stock Corporation Law itself and may still be amended on the basis of a pending uniform directive of the EEC authorities. The present Law includes provisions against excessive reserves, the over- or under-valuation of assets and for the proper accounting of liabilities. The annual financial statements with a business report containing much mandatory detail are established by the board of management, examined by auditors who must be elected by the shareholders' meeting each year, and further examined and approved by the supervisory board. The annual business report shall deal with the *AG's* relations to connected enterprises in some detail but this is not mandatory if they are domiciled abroad. Unless referred to the shareholders' meeting, the financial statements are therewith final and the shareholders' meeting decides only on the application of the profit.

Interim dividends

are not possible. The articles may provide, however, for an advance payment on the expected dividend prior to the resolution authorizing the dividend. This may be distributed only after the end of the respective fiscal year. Annual financial statements can be invalid for unjustified over- or under-valuation of assets or, in case of doubt, the court may order a special examination on demand of a shareholder minority.

Foreign stock corporations

must register their German branches. For such purpose the foreign corporation must show a fully committed, not merely

63

authorized, share capital of its own which as a rule requires at least the equivalent of the minimum applying to German stock corporations, i. e. *DM 100,000.* The branch, although a part of a corporation under foreign law, is subject to German labor law with regard to the representative institutions of employees (shop councils, economic council) in its German units, however it has no supervisory board.

CONNECTED ENTERPRISES *(Verbundene Unternehmen)*

Enterprises (not individuals) of whatever form, domestic or foreign, must file a notification in writing with respect to a domestic *AG* if they hold or have ceased to hold over 25 per cent or the majority of the *AG's* shares. The *AG* so notified must publish these facts. The membership rights following from such holdings cannot be exercised as long as the notification has not been made. An *AG* is itself similarly obligated with regard to its own participation in other *AGs, KGaAs, GmbHs* or mining corporations. The relations between connected enterprises, especially for a company-grouping under one directing enterprise, the

combine *(Konzern)*,

are subject to further detailed regulation in the interest of outside shareholders, creditors, and the general public; wholly owned subsidiaries are not excepted. In addition, the Stock Corporation Law of 1965 has created an entirely new type of combination of *AGs*,

integrated enterprises *(eingegliederte Gesellschaften)*,

which, by maintaining their corporate identities, has the effect of a reversible merger of an *AG* into another *AG.* The Law requires that such other *AG*, a domestic *AG*, holds all or 95 per cent of the shares of the "merging" *AG.*

Mutually participating enterprises *(wechselseitig beteiligte Unternehmen)*,

64

in which either an *AG* or *KGaA* is involved, are subject to certain limitations for the exercising of their mutual shareholding rights.

Certain contracts between enterprises *(Unternehmensverträge)* are subject to strict formalities and also to public disclosure. They include contracts by which an *AG* or *KGaA* subjects itself to the direction of another enterprise: contracts of domination *(Beherrschungsvertrag)*, or by which it agrees to transfer all or a part of its profits to another enterprise: contracts to transfer profits *(Gewinnabführungsvertrag)* – here tax provisions must be considered – or by which it agrees to pool all or part of its profit with another enterprise or to lease or otherwise transfer its business to another. For a combine involving a domestic *AG* or *KGaA*, the regulations differ depending upon whether or not the combine relations are formalized by an enterprise contract. The

combine by contract *(Vertragskonzern)*

– more precisely, a combine based on a contract of domination – authorizes the dominating enterprise to direct the dependent corporation in its general business or individual transactions, even to the latter's disadvantage, as long as this serves the overall interest of the combine. Within this system, the officers and the boards of the dominating and of the dependent enterprises are liable to the dependent corporation and its creditors for violations of their duties, apart from certain mandatory provisions of the contract securing the dependent corporation, its creditors and outside shareholders. If the relations between a controlling enterprise and the *AG* or *KGaA* are not so formalized by a contract, i. e. in the case of a so-called

de facto combine *(faktischer Konzern)*,

the dominating enterprise is not prohibited from giving directives, however, it may not thereby cause the dependent corporation to enter into transactions or to take or omit measures which are disadvantageous to it without providing adequate arm's length compensation. The dominating enterprise and its acting representatives are otherwise responsible for the resulting damage. The members of the boards of the dependent corporation are also responsible if they fail to render or to examine properly an annual report, commonly called a

report of dependence *(Abhängigkeitsbericht)*

which must be made by the board of management of the dependent corporation and which must list all transactions and measures taken or omitted at the initiative or in the interest of combine enterprises. The report must indicate the consideration received in these transactions, the reasons for measures or omissions and their advantages or disadvantages. The report is subject to audit and to examination by the dependent corporation's supervisory board. The latter's annual report to the shareholders' meeting must include certain statements on the result of such examination. The report itself is not published nor filed with any authority. However, every shareholder may ask the court for a separate examination if the statements made by the board of management, the auditors or the supervisory board contain reservations.

Consolidated financial statements

must include domestic enterprises of which the enterprise controlling a combine directly or indirectly owns more than one-half of the capital, except for negligible holdings. Such statements and explanatory business reports are required if the controlling enterprise of the combine is a domestic *AG* or *KGaA*, or if it is a domestic *GmbH* or mining corporation and one of the combine-enterprises is an *AG* or *KGaA*. So-called "consolidation in part" by the domestic *AG* or *KGaA* which is closest to the head of the combine is required if the head of the combine itself is not obligated to prepare consolidated financial statements by its legal structure or is foreign domiciled, provided in both cases that it controls other combine enterprises through one or more domestic *AGs* or *KGaAs*. Consolidation in part is also prescribed for a domestic *GmbH* or mining corporation if a combine head which itself is not obligated to prepare consolidated financial statements controls an *AG* or *KGaA* through such *GmbH* or mining corporation. A foreign domiciled combine head may dispense with consolidating and reporting on its domestic group if it publishes in the Federal Gazette consolidated financial statements which comply with the principles of the German regulations and which are examined by auditors. In order to make major business enterprises more transparent for the public benefit, a further statutory development (the *Publizitätsgesetz* – Disclosure Law) obligates

LARGE ENTERPRISES,

whatever their legal form (except co-operatives and some others) to account for, have audited and publish their annual financial data in a manner similar to stock corporations, if at least two of the following three criteria apply: a balance sheet total exceeding *DM* 125 million; sales exceeding *DM* 250 million; and an average employment of more than 5,000 persons. The criteria are different for banks and insurance companies: for banks a balance sheet total which exceeds *DM* 300 million including certain additional business data is necessary and, for insurance companies, proceeds from premiums exceeding *DM* 100 million suffice.

Consolidated financial statements must be made and audited and respective publications made by combines which are not already subject to the respective provisions of the Stock Corporation Law if their consolidated data meet the above criteria. If the head of the combine is not a domestic enterprise but if it dominates German enterprises through one or more enterprises in Germany, a consolidation in part of the German group must be established and the *Publizitätsgesetz* must be complied with, if the German group is within the above criteria. This is dispensed with if the foreign head of the combine publishes in the Federal Gazette its audited consolidated financial statements drawn up pursuant to the principles of the Stock Corporation Law.

Certain uniform disclosure requirements for

– applicable to stock corporations *(AG)* and companies with limited liability *(GmbH)* were enacted by Germany in 1969 following a directive of the Council of Ministers (1968) – a first step in complying with the harmonization of company laws as provided in the Treaty of the European Economic Community (EEC – Rome Treaty).

A second directive of the Council (1976) regulating the formation only of the stock corporation, its minimum capital and the preservation and alteration of the capital and some other provisions, has not yet been enacted, but German law complies already with the proposed principles. A number of further directives proposed by the Commission have made no progress sofar; they relate to mergers of stock corporations, to the annual accounting of corporations and of groups of companies, to detailed provisions for the structure of stock corporations, to the prospectus of securities' issues; planned is a scheme for inter-company relations following the German regulation for "connected enterprises". The proposal of the Commission in 1970 of a supranational European company (Societas Europae), based on plans, studies and drafts over a great many years, has been criticised as unnecessary and impractical by business, lawyers and the more realistic politicians of the member states. Agreed between member states, but not yet ratified and of little importance for Germany in view of already existing practice is a convention on the recognition of foreign corporations.

XI. SECURITIES AND STOCK EXCHANGES

ISSUE

The public or private offering and sale in Germany of securities issued outside of Germany by foreign companies requires no governmental approval.

Prior approval of the Federal Minister of Economics, however, is required for the issuance within Germany of negotiable bonds and debentures including convertible issues whether denominated in *Deutsche Mark* or a foreign currency. For this purpose, securities are normally deemed to be "issued" at the place stated in the bond or debenture provided there is good justification for such place in case it differs from the center of administration of the issuer.

No such approval is required for equity securities. A special regulatory authority, such as the US Securities and Exchange Commission, does not exist.

Public and private offerings of straight debt securities, whether denominated in *Deutsche Mark* or a foreign currency, issued within Germany are informally regulated, in particular as to timing and principal amount by the unofficial Central Capital Market Committee (*Zentraler Kapitalmarktausschuß*), a voluntary regulatory committee of some leading banks.

Offerings in Germany of straight debt securities denominated in *Deutsche Mark* but issued outside Germany are subject to informal regulation by a sub-committee of this committee if the securities shall be listed on a German stock exchange. This informal regulation would be applicable to any Euro-*DM* debt issue. The German managing underwriter notifies the Federal Association of German Banks which acts as secretary of the Central Capital Market Committee when the preliminary terms of an issue have been negotiated. Equity and convertible debt issues are not subject to such informal regulation.

At present no regulatory requirements apply to the

PUBLIC OFFERING

and sale of foreign securities in Germany, except in connection with stock exchange listings or, as noted below, in connection with the distribution of shares of foreign investment funds. Thus, no offering prospectus, circular or advertising is required for the offering and sale of securities to German banks, dealers or the general public. However, a draft bill is under discussion which is to introduce basically the same restrictions as are applicable in the case of shares of foreign investment funds.

Invitations for offers to purchase which are mailed to potential investors or published in newspapers need not comply with any specific laws or regulations. Door to door peddling and the soliciting of new clients by telephone is prohibited. No regulatory requirements apply to the

private offering

and sale in Germany of foreign securities of any kind.

PARTICULAR TRANSACTIONS

An offering of

Euro-bonds

issued by a foreign company does not require compliance with any German governmental regulation. An Euro-bond issue by a German company requires prior approval by the Federal Minister of Economics. The participation of German banks as underwriters or selling group members in a Euro-bond offering is not subject to any restrictions and requires no prior approval.

Rights offerings

by a foreign company to existing shareholders in the Federal Republic are not subject to any regulatory restrictions and require no governmental or other approval, unless such securities are listed on a German stock exchange, in which case certain stock exchange requirements must be observed. In particular, the foreign issuer must place an advertisement in the Federal Gazette and in one or more newspapers used for official publications by the German stock exchange announcing the beginning of the rights offering and supplying certain details relating thereto. In practice, this is handled by the German bank which originally sponsored the listing.

A secondary offering

of issues of outstanding securities of a foreign company is not subject to any regulatory restrictions and requires no governmental or other approval, whether or not the securities are listed on a German stock exchange; yet such secondary offerings are rather rare in Germany.

A public offering, in statutory language "the distribution . . . by way of public offer, public advertisement or solicitation or in a similar manner" in Germany of

shares in foreign investment funds,

may only be made if the fund complies with the fairly extensive provisions of the German Law on Foreign Investment Shares of 1969 *(AuslInvestmG)*. A notification to the Federal Banking Authority is required. Non-public, or private, offerings of such shares may be made without any restriction. However, there is a substantial tax disadvantage for German investors in investing in shares of foreign funds which do not comply with the Foreign Investment Law or which are not listed on a German stock exchange and for which a tax representative has not been appointed in Germany. In general

TRADING

in Germany of foreign securities is not restricted. Dealings can be effected through private communications, dealers, banks, brokers or stock exchanges, as applicable or desired by the parties.

STOCK EXCHANGES

Stock exchanges – too many – exist in Berlin, Bremen, Düsseldorf, Frankfurt, Hamburg, Hannover, Munich and Stuttgart. They are supervised by the states *(Börsenaufsicht)*. Listing on an exchange may be in two forms: official listing *(amtliche Notiz)* or semi-official listing *(geregelter Freiverkehr)*. If official listing is desired, a prescribed procedure must be followed. This requires the preparation of a prospectus. The listing prospectus is set up by the sponsoring bank in co-operation with the issuer; it will give a description of the legal status of the issuer; his financial position, earnings situation and business activities. These facts are, as a rule, based upon information already made available to the public by the issuer according to the laws and rules of his home state. According to German stock exchange regulations, the balance sheet to be

71

incorporated into the prospectus must not be older than eight months when the listing application is filed unless interim figures (in general not older than three months) are furnished. In this instance, the balance sheet may date back thirteen months. In case of the listing of a public issue, the prospectus must state also the purpose and the terms and conditions of the loan. The Common Market Commission in 1973 has issued a draft guide line providing for uniform rules on the information to be given in listing prospectuses.

Upon conclusion of the listing procedure, the prospectus in the version approved by the Stock Exchange Admission Board is published in the Federal Gazette, and, for each stock exchange where the bonds are to be listed, in a newspaper authorized for such publications. The annual financial statements of the issuer, as well as notices for the drawings of bonds, convocation of general assemblies etc., must be published in one authorized paper for each stock exchange as long as the listing is continued.

CIVIL LIABILITY

A purchaser who aquires the securities from the underwriters or members of the selling group may recover damages against

the issuer

only upon proof that the issuer acted deliberately and intentionally to cause loss to the purchaser. Negligence alone is not sufficient. In addition, the issuance of an official prospectus in connection with a stock exchange listing may involve certain statutory liabilities for the issuer in respect to the accuracy of the information in the prospectus. Such liability will exist over a period of five years after listing with respect to purchase contracts upon proof that there was an inaccurate statement of a material fact of which the issuer either had knowledge, or but for his gross negligence would have had knowledge, or that there was an omission of a material fact, which omission is based on malicious concealment. If there is no stock exchange listing in Germany, the only civil liability of the issuer that can arise from a prospectus is the liability referred to above for deliberate and intentional action.

and members of the selling group who sell securities in Germany will be liable if the rights incorporated in the security sold are not in existence or if a procedure to invalidate the security has been initiated. Except for special circumstances, the seller is not liable for the value of the security. In any case, a purchaser could hold a member of the selling group liable upon proof that the underwriter acted deliberately and intentionally to cause loss to the purchaser. Negligence alone would not be a basis for an action against a seller. Underwriters who form part of a syndicate which applies for a listing of securities on a German stock exchange are subject to the same statutory liabilities as the issuer, referred to above, for the accuracy of the information in the listing prospectus. Only German banks and foreign banks having German branches may be members of such a syndicate, provided the bank in question is admitted to a German stock exchange.

CRIMINAL LIABILITY

If the seller or persons responsible for the prospectus act fraudulently, they are subject to punishment pursuant to respective provisions of the Stock Exchange Law *(Börsengesetz)*.

INSIDER RULES

Rules on insider trading are provided not by statute or regulation but by voluntary commitments of the various organizations and companies concerned; rules were recommended first in 1970 by a commission of stock exchange experts appointed by the Federal Minister of Finance.

XII. TRADE PRACTICES, CARTELS, MARKET DOMINATION

Business and the public generally are protected against unfair trade practices *(unlauterer Wettbewerb)* and, with exceptions, against restraint of trade and monopoly *(Wettbewerbsbeschränkungen)*. These two fields of trade practices are treated separately in German law. Their interrelation is growing. The first field is a traditional field of law as in all jurisdictions of the Western world. The second field originated as a US import of the post-war period but took a development of its own pursuant to German legal notions. In the first field, the prosecution of offences is left to business itself, trade associations and consumer associations, while in the second field, apart from private litigation, government agencies are in charge.

The principle that unlawful practices will be checked or policed only insofar as effects occur within the Federal Republic of Germany is strictly applied to restraint of trade. German courts will, however, protect a German national against unfair trade practices committed abroad by another German national. It has also been decided that the advertisement in Germany with respect to a consumer market across the border must comply with German fair trade law. The European Commission has drafted guide lines for fair trade in the Community, and as a result of its jurisdiction regarding the foreign trade of the Community it has protected, in some cases since 1977, the business of the Community against dumping practices of importers. Germany has undertaken in some

INTERNATIONAL AGREEMENTS

expressly to include foreign nationals under her protection, for example, in the provisions of the Paris Agreement on Protection of Industrial Property (Union Convention) for the suppression of unfair trade practices. The German-American Treaty of Friendship, Commerce and Navigation provides for consultation in the field of restraint of trade. More practical might become a supplementary agreement entered into by both governments in 1976 for the cooperation of the mutual administrative agencies (not included is mutual judicial aid in such cases). The German government's efforts of cooperation with the cartel authorities of other states including Japan continue as well as German participation in the work of international organizations for the control of restrictive practices in world trade. Directly applicable to business enterprises are provisions of the treaty establishing the European Coal and Steel Community (*Montanunion,* concluded 1951) and of the treaty establishing the European Economic Community (concluded 1957 in Rome: Rome Treaty).

UNFAIR TRADE PRACTICES

Fair competition among business enterprises under German law is governed by several statutes and much case law. The rules cover the entire range of unfair competitive practices such as unfair or deceptive means of trading and commercial advertising, and boycott. The number and substance of the various activities which have been held to be illegal indicate that the general attitude of the courts has been towards an increasing refinement of distinctions between fair and unfair practices. The law of advertising is stricter than under Anglo-American law. When doing business in Germany, foreign enterprises should make sure to check each one of their proposed activities before applying them in the market. The principal statute in this field, the Law against Unfair Competition (*Gesetz gegen den unlauteren Wettbewerb: UWG*) contains the basic definition of unfair trade practices, a so-called

general clause,

that condemns any business action undertaken for the purpose of competition and which violates "good morals". Such action may be stopped and the offender may be made liable for damages. While there are a few further special definitions of offensive acts, the great majority of the cases in this field must be defined by interpretation of the general clause. The compatibility with "good morals" is defined by the ethics of reasonable and honest businessmen or of that part of the public which is affected by the competing parties. Owing to its vagueness, the general clause must be read in the light of decided cases.

In advertising

the competitors must offer their products and services in the market without influencing the customers' independent judgment and free choice through persuasive statements which are not justified by, and inherent in, the advertised products or services themselves. Customers shall not be unduly allured or intruded on their free decision by obliging them morally to buy the merchandise offered.

False representations

The chief requirement under German law for all advertising is that the statements made are true. This applies to quality, origin, price, quantity and all other data on goods which are apt to influence the decision to make the bargain. Also, statements are banned which – though literally true – are likely to be erroneously read by the customer as offering certain advantages. This may apply where qualitites are unduly emphasized or where terms are used which have an ambiguous meaning.

Comparative advertising

While it is recognized that competiton by its nature involves a sound measure of rivalry between conflicting trade interests, the rule is that advertising should rest solely upon the qualities of the product to be sold and refrain from any reference to the competitor and his products. It is strictly forbidden to expressly mention a competitor's name or product. The same is true for personal attacks on competitors, even if not expressly named; an example would be the statement that a competitor is a foreigner. Also an attack, if directed against a certain category of competitors in a general way only (drug stores, department stores, all manufacturers of a certain article), would be considered unfair.

Perhaps the most frequent reference to a competitor is made by comparison of his goods with one's own goods as to quality, price, or achieved results. Any such comparison, express or implied, is permitted only if it is justified under the circumstances of the individual case, e. g. if the statements describing the characteristics of the advertised goods are true and presented objectively and provide a complete picture of the goods in question. The comparison of prices might be permissible under special circumstances, such as in the case of goods of the same manufacturer which are priced differently by the local trade.

A government bill proposes to amend the UWG by a right to rescind the contract and to damages for persons who entered into the contract as a result of unfair advertising. The European Commission has submitted to the Council of Ministers a draft ordinance on misleading and unfair advertising.

Of some importance in practice are

extra advantages

offered as incentives to buy. Such offers may under certain conditions be illegal. The typical cases in question may roughly be divided into gifts, price reductions, special sales and price events. If

gifts

are connected with the sale of merchandise to customers or with an advertising campaign to the public, it must be carefully ascertained in each case whether the advantage offered with the sale or for the purpose of advertising is permissible. If gifts are offered or granted to the buyer on the condition of a purchase, a special ordinance (Zugabe-Verordnung) applies. Only gifts specified in this ordinance are permitted, e. g. if they are of insignificant value or pertinent accessories usually granted without an additional charge to the customer. They may, however, in no case be stated to constitute "gifts" or to be given gratuitously. Additional merchandise of the same kind or cash may be given in connection with a purchase only to customers other than ultimate consumers.

Where the advertised merchandise itself is given away, it should be no more than a distribution of samples. The quantity should not exceed the reasonable minimum required for test purposes by the customer. Free distribution of normal size items, therefore, is permitted only if smaller samples would not sufficiently serve the purpose.

As a general rule, the seller is free in the

pricing

of his goods. Resale price maintenance for brand name goods, an old tradition of German fair trade law, has been abolished except for books, magazines and newspapers in 1973 by an amendment of the Cartel Law with the permission to "recommend" resale prices if it is stated expressly that such recommendation is not binding. Government price regulation still exists in a few protected areas.

Rebates

– price reductions – if offered or granted with the sale of everyday goods to the ultimate consumer are subject to a special statute *(Rabattgesetz)*. Such rebates, as a rule, may not exceed three per cent of the offered purchase price, nor exceed quantity rebates of commercial usage in the case of quantity purchases. It is not permitted to offer or grant rebates or special prices to certain groups only of ultimate consumers.

Special Sales

and similar actions of retailers are permissible or permitted in rare cases only. Sales for the reason of either the closing of a business altogether or for the giving up certain classes of goods require a government permit. No permit is required for seasonal sales during predetermined dates.

Lottery and quiz

A lottery is illegal and a punishable offence under the German Penal Code if it is not entirely gratuitous. Non-gratuitous lotteries include those where participation is made dependent on the purchase of tickets or merchandise (coupons on wrapping etc.). Gratuitous lotteries, prize puzzles and quizes are permitted in principle unless they offer excessive prizes and if the participation is not subject to the purchase of goods.

The private sphere

of the individual is protected. Thus the soliciting of customers by telephone, telex and under certain circumstances unrequested visits by agents, have been held to constitute an unfair trade practice. A customer may revoke his obligation under any instalment sale without giving reasons or suffering disadvantages, within a brief interval after his signature.

Trade names

are protected under several provisions of law. The most frequently applied provision is contained in the *UWG* and guards against the use of a name, a firm, or the specific designation of a business enterprise or marketing activity which is likely to cause confusion with the name, the firm or the specific designation which another enterprise lawfully uses. On a smaller local scale, this same objective of protecting enterprises and customers against the confusion of similar names is accomplished through the Commercial Code which provides that each new firm name must clearly differ from all firm names already existing and filed with the Commercial Register at the same place or in the same region. This rule is also applied to subsidiaries of existing enterprises in new localities. A conflict between confusingly similar names will, as a rule, be decided by the criteria of public recognition and priority of use of either name. If the designation of a business is simply letters or part of the general vocabulary, it may nevertheless be protected if it can be distinctly shown that it has sufficient commercial recognition by the general public (AEG, IBM). If the recognition of a firm name or sign is unique as with some world-renowned firms, protection is granted even against non-competing firms. As a matter of fair trade, important sounding name elements such as "works", "international", "euro...", "deutsch..." are permissible only for enterprises whose size or scope justifies such a designation.

Other Acts of Unfair Competition

The *UWG* defines other violations of a civil or criminal nature outside the areas of sales or advertising: bribery of employees of another enterprise in order to obtain advantages in the purchase of goods or services; slander against another's business; and disclosure of business secrets by employees for the purposes of competition, or profit-making or damaging the principal; and the use for the same purpose of information received in such a way by others. It is, as a rule, illegal to intentionally induce a customer or an employee or another person to break his agreement with a competitor. But it is legal to hire employees of a competitor, provided the employees give regular notice of termination of their service contracts unless this is done systematically to harm the competitor.

RESTRAINTS OF COMPETITION

The German post-war law, the Law against Restraints of Competition *(Gesetz gegen Wettbewerbsbeschränkungen, GWB,* commonly called *Kartellgesetz)* has been in effect since January 1, 1958, which was also the effective date of the "rules of competiton" of the Rome Treaty. After several amendments over the years, major amendments were introduced again in 1973, mainly by adding concerted action in restraint of trade to the prohibited forms of collective restraints, by abolishing resale price maintenance for branded goods (books, magazines and newspapers still excepted), by stricter controls as to restrictive clauses in vertical agreements while facilitating cooperation between smaller business enterprises, by a broader definition of market dominating enterprises and, most important, by the introduction of controls of mergers and other forms of enterprise concentration, and by the establishment of an advisory commission of independent experts.

Except for cases of only regional significance attended to by state authorities and the rare cases of the jurisdiction of the Federal Minister of Economics, a separate federal high authority is charged with the administration and enforcement of the Law, the

FEDERAL CARTEL OFFICE *(Bundeskartellamt, BKA)*

in Berlin. Because the *GWB* reversed the German traditional cartel notions, the authorities were faced with the problem of adaptation and education of the business community. They acted with consideration from the beginning. In the meantime, the administrative practice is firm and the courts have decided a number of controversial points. Legal literature on the subject is overabundant.

The *BKA* annually renders a comprehensive report which covers all developments and activities in the field giving full statistics of the enforcement of the many sections of the Law. Included is a report on the practice and developments under the Rome Treaty. The report is preceded by an opinion of the federal government, is submitted to the parliament and published.

Apart from the exemption of certain fields of economic activity, the *GWB* applies to all restraints of competition between enterprises whether created by agreement, concerted action, unilateral measures or simply resulting from the force of events.

The *GWB* is mandatory public law. It applies to all restraints of competition which are effective within the Federal Republic of Germany, even if they are caused from abroad. The administration is held to prosecute offences but the public interest may justify exceptions. The jurisdiction is not, however, extended to actions of German enterprises abroad, unless these foreign activities affect competition in Germany.

Different regulations apply to horizontal and vertical restraints of competition. Certain types of restraints are, or may be, permitted. The misuse of monopoly, oligopoly or market domination is prohibited.

81

are defined generally as "agreements concluded by enterprises or associations of enterprises for a joint purpose and resolutions of associations of enterprises which are apt to influence, through restraints of competition, the production or market conditions for dealing in goods or commercial services". After some controversy whether this definition covers only expressly agreed – to restraints or also restraints which are merely the consequence of an agreement the Federal Supreme Court has terminated this controversy by deciding, in 1975, that not only such restraints are covered by this definition which are expressly stipulated in the agreement but that agreements are also prohibited if the restraint of trade is the consequence of the agreement and if the parties, even tacitly, have approved of that consequence.

Agreements and resolutions covering

uniform general business conditions
(Konditionenkartelle)

are permitted upon application to the cartel authorities. These agreements may include terms of delivery, warranties and payment, cash discounts *(Skonti)*, but not the fixing of prices or price elements. Trade associations may recommend the application of uniform general business conditions including terms of payment (not prices); they must expressly be stated as not binding and no pressure of any kind may be exercised for their use. The cartel authority may intervene in the case of abuses. Under the same conditions associations of small and medium-sized enterprises may recommend business conditions including prices if this serves to promote the efficiency of their members in relation to large enterprises and to improve thereby the conditions of competition. Agreements and resolutions covering

uniform rebates *(Rabattkartelle)*

are permitted in connection with the delivery of goods provided the rebates represent genuine consideration and do not lead to

82

unjustified discrimination under certain conditions. Permitted are also agreements on or recommendations of

uniform industrial standards
(Normen- und Typenkartelle)

if supported by the competent expert association. Under special circumstances, which include due consideration of the economy in general as well as the public interest, the cartel authority may permit a cartel designed to bridge a structural crisis within an industry by an adaptation of the capacities to the demand – the so-called

Strukturkrisenkartell.

Cartels with the objective of rationalizing economic processes

Rationalisierungskartelle

may be permitted if it can be shown that they will substantially promote the efficiency or economy of the participating enterprises and improve the supply of the market, provided these advantages are in a reasonable relation to the restraint of competition arising as a result of the cartel. Under such conditions even price fixing arrangements and syndicates (joint institutions for sale or procurement) can be permitted, if the advantages cannot be reached by other means and if the cartel is in the public interest.

Spezialisierungskartelle

– agreements and resolutions calling for the specialization of enterprises are permitted if substantial competition in the market can still be shown. In such cases, even joint distribution agencies have been permitted.
To promote their efficiency small and medium-sized enterprises are encouraged to rationalize by cooperation provided that the competition in the market is not thereby impaired. Where

offers are solicited

and an examination of the offers can only be made on the basis of a description of the tender or the breakdown of the price, agreements on uniform methods of describing the tender or the breakdown of prices are permitted if the agreements contain no fixing of prices or price elements.

Export cartels

which are limited to the regulation of foreign markets are permitted. No confirming decision of the cartel authority is necessary. If the export cartel affects competition within Germany also, the cartel may be permitted by the cartel authorities under certain conditions, unless the cartel violates an international treaty to which Germany is a party. Under the same conditions,

import cartels

may be permitted if German importers are not confronted with substantial competition between the sellers.

Ministerkartelle.

A cartel may be allowed in the interest of prevailing reasons of the whole of the economy or under singular conditions to meet an immediate danger to the major part of a business branch. In such unique cases, the Federal Minister of Economics himself acts as the cartel authority.
The ancillary clause of a contract stipulating

the prohibition to compete *(Wettbewerbsverbot)*

is allowed in the case of the sale of a business to the extent the freedom of the seller is not inequitably limited, and under respective conditions in employment- and agency (distributor) agreements even for a time after the expiration of such agreements.

84

Frequency of permitted cartels

Much use has been made particularly in the first years of the Cartel Law's application of cartels covering uniform business conditions and uniform rebates – the two are often combined – and of export cartels. Specialization cartels and cooperative rationalization of small and medium-sized enterprises are used to some extent. Other cartel forms are less frequent.
The wider reaching forms of rationalization cartels are not readily permitted. They were refused in the cases of some traditional German syndicates for the distribution of basic materials.

VERTICAL AGREEMENTS

between enterprises restricting competition are subject to different regulations, depending on the type of restrictions. The

fixing of prices

and business conditions for resale is void except that resale price maintenance is still permitted for books, magazines and newspapers.
The mere recommendation of resale prices for brand name goods by the manufacturer is permitted under certain conditions if the recommendation is expressly designated as being not binding. The Federal Cartel Office may still intervene, e. g. if the recommendation leads to prices not justified by the general conditions of the economy or if the recommended price exceeds in a majority of cases the actual prices in the market. Price leadership entails no advantages.

Price reporting systems

and exchange of detailed market information are often a cause of investigation and in recent years rarely passed by the cartel authority. They are considered as illegal if they have the "effect of weakening the competitive activity" of the participants.

Other vertical tying clauses – for example tie-in sales, obligations to purchase raw materials from a certain source, exclusivity clauses in distributorship agreements and the like – are in principle valid, but the cartel authority may interfere for a number of statutory reasons, in particular if the restraints turn out to prevent other enterprises from entering the market. This principle also applies to restrictions imposed on a seller or licensor in agreements for the sale or

license of patents.

Limitations imposed on the purchaser or licensee which go beyond the scope of the patent grant are, in principle, prohibited. Exceptions apply, for example, to clauses which require a certain pricing for patented goods, or to the licensee's obligation to exchange experience or to grant the licensor rights to improvements (grant backs) if such obligations correspond to similar but not necessarily equal obligations of the licensor. Other tying clauses on the licensee may be permitted if they are reasonable and do not substantially restrain the competiton in the market. Agreements on the sale or license of

know-how

are recognized, subject to the same principles and to the extent that the know-how is secret.

ENFORCEMENT OF PERMITTED CARTELS, FORMALITIES

Permitted cartels and vertical restraints of competiton are enforceable in courts. Cartels and vertical agreements must be in writing. Security which has been pledged by the participants of a cartel to guard against violations of the cartel agreement may not be utilized, however, unless the cartel authority has given special permission. Permitted cartels are entered into a public register, with the exception of mere export cartels. Certain applications to, and decisions by, the cartel authority require publication. In some cases, the trade concerned must be heard. All permitted cartel agreements and other permitted restrictions remain under the supervision of the cartel authority, which may intervene in case of misuse. The authority may conduct investigations at the enterprises, request information and conduct administrative proceedings. In addition, the *BKA* has developed a practice of advising enterprises informally of its objections, discussing the matter and even settling issues if agreement can be reached. Every formal decision of the cartel authority may be appealed to an ordinary court, the *Oberlandesgericht* which is competent in the cartel authority's district. A further appeal to the Federal Supreme Court on questions of law may be allowed.

MONOPOLY, OLIGOPOLY, MARKET DOMINATION
(marktbeherrschende Unternehmen)

Domination of a market is held to exist if an enterprise is not faced with material competiton for a certain kind of goods or services, or by an amended definition of 1973 if the enterprise has a "superior market position" not only by its market share but also by its financial strength or from other factors which may affect the entry of other enterprises into the market. Market domination exists also to the extent two or more enterprises in their entirety fulfil the above conditions. In the case of certain market shares market domination is assumed. The cartel authority, after hearing the enterprises, may prohibit abusive actions, such as excessive pricing, and may declare abusive agreements of market dominating enterprises ineffective.

CONTROL OF MERGERS AND ACQUISITIONS
(Zusammenschlüsse, Fusionskontrolle).

Mergers, acquisitions, joint ventures and certain other arrangements of taking influence on other enterprises as defined by the Law must be reported to the *BKA*. After the 1973 amendment, the *BKA* may prohibit the transaction if it can be expected that the transaction results in the creation or strengthening of a market dominating position, unless the parties can show that the transaction will also result in improvements of the competitive situation and that such improvements outweigh the disadvantages of market domination. Apart from the right to appeal against such a decision to the courts (as against any other decision of any cartel authority) the Law allows in this case a special application of the parties to the transaction to the Federal Minister of Economics. He may still approve the transaction if the restraints of competition are compensated for by overall economic advantages of the transaction, or if the latter is justified by an overriding public interest. Transactions of a minor importance are exempt from reporting and interference by the cartel authorities. Transactions of a major size or having otherwise substantial effect on the market as defined in the Law must be reported even before they are entered into (preventive merger control); they become valid if the *BKA* does not prohibit them within a statutory period. Divestitures are sometimes suggested by the *BKA* and followed to obtain approval of the transaction. A

MONOPOLY COMMISSION
(Monopolkommission)

of independent experts was created in 1973 with advisory functions only. It has a record, however, already of noteworthy contributions. The Commission comments and advises in the area of business concentration, on the administration of the Law and on amendments which it considers to be desirable.

CERTAIN UNILATERAL ACTIONS

are prohibited including boycotts, the use of threats or promises to cause another enterprise to violate the Law or an order of the cartel authority, the forcing of another enterprise to join even a permitted cartel or to combine in a market controlling enterprise, or the forcing of another enterprise to accept attitudes conforming to those of others for the purpose of restraining competition. The Law does not require every enterprise to deal with every bona fide customer. An obligation to contract with such customer and the prohibition of discrimination

as well as the prohibition to hinder another enterprise inequitably in exploiting its competitive business activity applies, however, to market controlling enterprises and enterprises or associations of enterprises which benefit from permits or exemptions under the Law, including enterprises or their associations on whose merchandise or services other enterprises are dependent without adequate and reasonably accessible other sources. Even such enterprises are in principle free to choose their own distribution channels; an exception has been made for certain goods whose sale requires no service, such as film. It has been held that a leading automobile manufacturer violates the non-discrimination provision by refusing to supply an autoleasing firm while supplying a competitor leasing firm owned by the manufacturer.

Codes of ethics for fair competition
(Wettbewerbsregeln)

may be issued by business associations within the scope of the GWB and the Law against Unfair Competition and related statutes. They constitute rules regulating the conduct of enterprises in competition in order to counteract conduct which contravenes the principles of fair competition and the effectiveness of competition; the rules are to stimulate competition pursuant to such principles. The proceedings provide for the hearing of the businesses affected by such codes, and a public hearing may be called.

ENFORCEMENT OF THE GWB, FINES AND DAMAGES

An offence is committed, in particular if a person purposely disregards the invalidity of prohibited cartels, or acts purposely against other prohibitions of the Law, or purposely has recommended an actual violation or evasion of the Law. Fines for offences are assessed by the cartel authority, but the offender may apply for a judicial decision. The BKA has become increasingly active by imposing substantial fines on major enterprises and on certain of their responsible officers personally. Offences violating the Law are not of a criminal nature. Any person may claim actually sustained

damages

incurred by an intentional or negligent violation of the Law or of orders made under the Law. The courts are to inform the *BKA* of all cases concerning disputes in cartel matters. The *BKA* may participate in such proceedings.

EXEMPTIONS FROM THE LAW

The statutory definition of cartels excludes completely the fields of labor agreements and public services such as social insurance. Exempt without limitations is the Federal Bank *(Bundesbank)* and the state central banks *(Landeszentralbanken)* which in spite of their name are branches of the Federal Bank. Also exempt are the alcohol monopoly and the match monopoly to the extent their services and prices are regulated by law.

A great volume of economic activity is exempt from cartel law to the extent that special regulations exist in other laws, and, in a number of cases, on the condition that the cartel authority may intervene in case of a misuse of the freedom gained by the exemption. Where a special supervisory authority exists for certain business, the intervention of the cartel authority requires contact with or the concurrence of these supervisory authorities. This covers e. g. the mails and the services for public transportation as regulated by such special authorities as well as the business of banking, insurance, building-loan savings banks, and agreements of public utilities for electricity, gas and water.

EUROPEAN CARTEL LAW

As to coal and steel, and products pertaining thereto under the European Coal and Steel Community Treaty, the cartel and price law of the Treaty replaces national law; here the European Commission has been quite liberal in allowing concentration of the steel industry and very recently protected it against dumping from abroad.

The "rules of competition" regarding other industries and trades, however, do not replace national law: they apply to interstate commerce only, i. e. to the trade between member states. These rules are contained in two broad articles of the Rome Treaty. These articles have been supplemented to some extent by ordinances and constitute directly applicable law.

The EEC Commission is entrusted with the enforcement of EEC law. The Commission has the right to direct information from the enterprises, but keeps close contact with the respective national cartel authorities. The authority's decisions are appealable to a court, the European Court of Justice.

The Rome Treaty follows largely the concept and techniques utilized in German law – the prohibition, in principle, of cartels between independent enterprises, with the possibility of exemptions under certain conditions; and the prohibition of the misuse of market domination, but with no divestiture. But the view of the Commission that the acquisition of competitors by a market dominating enterprise may constitute a misuse of market domination and is therefore void has been accepted by the European Court of Justice. The Commission has prepared a draft of an ordinance for the control of mergers and acquisitions and an amended draft of the ordinance on sole distributorships.

In some aspects, European cartel law is more strict than German law. This applies in particular to the practice of the Commission (still untried by the Court) with regard to joint ventures, and to restrictive clauses in license agreements, expecially to its negative views as to exclusive, and territorially limited licenses. This latter attitude has met for years the criticism of the industries concerned, also of governments, and is the reason that the acceptance of drafts of the Commission for an ordinance of the Council of Ministers permitting certain types of restrictive clauses in license agreements is being delayed.

The principle that cartels, vertical restrictions of competition and the misuse of market domination are prohibited generally has been modified to the extent that agreements or measures of a restrictive nature which are timely reported may be practiced until the Commission has rendered a decision to the contrary; such a decision may have a retroactive effect in the field of civil liability. The European Court of Justice as well as the Commission have applied a kind of a rule of reason in order to promote desirable co-operation between enterprises and in order to concentrate on major violations of the principles of the Rome Treaty. Consequently, violations of the Treaty are not prohibited if the market position of the parties concerned is altogether too weak to result in a noticeable restraint of trade. In a case involving major violations of the rules of competition of the Rome Treaty by foreign (outside of the Common Market domiciled) enterprises the European Court of Justice has confirmed the application of the rules to foreign enterprises as well as the validity of service of process in such cases on a Common-Market-subsidiary of the foreign enterprise.

Conflict between national and European cartel law

The European Court of Justice has decided that pending EEC proceedings are no impediment to the institution of proceedings by a national cartel authority of a member state in the same matter, provided the national proceedings and measures do not affect or impair European law, or EEC proceedings and measures. In assessing a fine the Commission has refused to make allowance for a fine already assessed in the same issue by US authorities.

It may be noted here that most member states have some legislation and exercise some control of cartels, restraints of competition, in particular of the pricing by dominant firms and some also of mergers. France rather encourages French owned or controlled mergers by looking not so much at its domestic market but at the worldmarket and at large American firms or concerns. Germany has by far the most comprehensive and detailed law and practice.

INTRA-ENTERPRISE

restraints of competition, i.e. restraints between parent and subsidiary or between subsidiaries at the directive of the parent, are, in practice, recognized as being legal under European as well as German law, provided the relationships are clearly based on corporate control.

CO-OPERATION

between independent enterprises to promote their competitive potential is encouraged. Such possibilities have been defined in some practical detail by the German Federal Minister of Economics and, to a lesser extent, by the EEC Commission. The co-operation manuals are designed particularly to serve small business without, however, being so restricted. German law recognizes manifold forms of cooperation among enterprises which serve rationalization and which do not fall under the provisions of the cartel law. In fact, cooperation agreements play an important role in practice. They relate, inter alia, to joint market research and market investigation, comparisons between businesses *(Betriebsvergleiche)* and industries *(Branchenvergleiche)*.

In particular, cooperation on or the establishment of joint facilities for purchase, distribution, research and development are subject matters of cooperation agreements. Such cooperation agreements may not result in any restriction on competition. This means, for instance, that enterprises utilizing joint facilities for purchase, distribution, or research may not agree with each other on the exclusive use of such facilities.

CARTEL LAW REFORM

is an ever current subject. The German trend is on improvement of the provisions relating to market dominating enterprises and merger control for the general objective to keep the economy competitive, and also to aid smaller and middle sized enterprises.

XIII. PATENTS, TRADEMARKS, LICENSES

Any foreign national may acquire patents, utility models, or trademarks subject to the same regulations as apply to German nationals. The Federal Republic of Germany participates in a great number of multinational and bilateral

CONVENTIONS

in this field. The classic ones are: The Paris Convention for the Protection of Industrial Property (Union Convention) of 1883 (repeatedly revised) which contains the right to claim priority of patent or trademark filings in member states and to which also Great Britain and the United States are parties and the Madrid Convention on the international registration of trademarks pursuant to the respective national laws of 1891 (repeatedly revised), in which neither Great Britain nor the United States participate.

The 1954 German-American Friendship Treaty contains provisions for patents and trademarks and there is an older special German-American treaty of 1909 on the mutual protection of industrial property. Apart from general regulations for Germany regarding the war- and post-war periods, there are some special regulations for international cooperation in matters such as defense or the peaceful use of atomic energy.

The European Court of Justice recognizes that the validity and scope of industrial property rights granted under national law is unaffected by the rules of competition of the Rome Treaty but does not exclude the latter's application to certain practices in the exercising of such rights.

After many years of difficult consultations and negotiations, some under the guidance of the World Intellectual Property Organization (WIPO) encouraging progress was achieved in transnational efforts to harmonize the national patent laws and to simplify patent applications.

After the European Convention on Requirements of Form for Patent Applications (1953) and on Patent Classification (1954), and amending Strassburg Conventions on patent classification and on the unification of some points of substantive patent law, the European Patent Convention for granting simultaneously by a single procedure a "bundle" of individual national patents, each governed by national law, became effective on October 7, 1977. It was ratified and properly documented to that date by seven of the sixteen signatory states: Germany, France, Great Britain, the Netherlands, Luxembourg, Belgium and Switzerland. But the Convention on a unique supranational patent law and procedure of the European Community (signed in Luxemburg in December 1975 by representatives of the nine member states) will only come into effect when everyone of the nine signatory states has ratified the convention; this will still take some time.

A world-wide Patent Cooperation Treaty (PCT), which provides for the filing of a patent in one partner state with effect also in any desired number of other partner states, has been signed in 1970 by 35 states, including Germany, the United States and Great Britain. The PCT has become effective in Germany on January 28, 1978. Its system respects and will cooperate with other regional patent arrangements such as the European Patent Convention.

As a result of these efforts, only one uniform text will be needed for one invention for national as well as for European or for PCT patent applications. Substantial saving of costs, identical scope of the patent claims throughout the industrial world, extremely simplified procedures will benefit industries of all interested states. It is expected that the administration of patent applications under the European convention at the European office in Munich and under the PCT at the German Patent Office in Munich shall begin in June or July 1978.

The German Patent Law, amended late in 1976, to conform to the new treaties' conditions will govern all applications filed after January, 1, 1978. Under German law, as amended,

PATENT APPLICATIONS

must be filed with the Patent Office (*Patentamt*) by the inventor or else the applicant must state his right to claim a patent for the invention, for example by operation of the Law on Employee

95

Inventions or by assignment from the inventor. The inventor must be named within three months after the filing. If there are two or more independent inventors, the first applicant has the sole right to the patent. A person who is thus precluded, but who has used or prepared to use the invention independently of another prior to the latter's filing date, may continue the free use of his invention, without formal process of law, but for his own purposes only. This right of prior reduction to practice is assignable or may be inherited only together with the original business in which the invention is used. If a person has applied for a patent without having acquired the right to do so from the true inventor, the latter may demand the transfer of the application or resulting patent. Any applicant without residence in Germany must appoint a resident attorney or patent attorney.

Contrary to earlier limitations food stuffs and other articles of consumption, pharmaceuticals and new matter as such resulting from a chemical process (*Stoffschutz*) may be patented. While microbiological processes and resulting products may be patented the protection of the invention of new plants or cultivating processes can be sought only under a special Law which was enacted in consequence of Germany's ratification of the International Convention for the Protection of Plant Cultivation of 1961.

Deferred examination

is applicable. Every application is examined for obvious defects. An examination of the merits of the application or a search as to novelty is no more done ex officio but only if requested by the applicant or any third party. If no motion for an examination of the merits is made within seven years after the filing of the application, or if the annual fee has not been paid in time, the application is deemed to have been withdrawn. All applications are laid open for public inspection eighteen months after the application or the priority date. As of that time the application enjoys a certain preliminary protection. The Law also regulates in all necessary detail the right to inspect the patent office files by anybody or in certain cases by a party showing a justified interest.

The Law does not provide for preliminary applications; subsequent amendments to an application which cannot be supported by the first disclosure of the invention may only be allowed as new separate applications. The application must specify the technical problem to be solved and the means of solving it in a way that a person with average expertise in the field is able to work with the patent. The invention must lend itself to commercial utilization and involve an inventive step,

Erfindungshöhe,

the requirement, in addition to novelty, of a creative level of the invention over and above the achievement of an ordinary expert. This "inventive step", a German specialty, was accepted by the other treaty partners in agreeing to certain uniform law provisions.

SCOPE OF A PATENT

Conforming to the European and PCT treaties the amended German Law determines the extent of the patent protection only by the terms of the patent claims as interpreted by the description and, – if applicable – by drawings or examples. This important development marks a major sacrifice to international uniformity of German legal tradition. To the extent patents and patent applications are still governed by the traditional law (i. e. applications before January 1, 1978) the courts will accordingly not adhere too strictly to the wording used in the patent, but investigate constructively the inventive idea as shown in the description, examples, drawings and claims of the patent as a whole. There is even the legal concept, and in consequence the legal protection, of a general inventive idea *(allgemeiner Erfindungsgedanke)* over and above the strict wording of the claims as they may be interpreted from the description *(unmittelbarer Gegenstand der Erfindung)*, especially in case of pioneer patents.

In addition to amendments as a result of litigation a provision of the 1968 amendment to the Law enables the holder of a patent to apply for a correction of the patent claims with retroactive effect.

INFRINGEMENT

is interpreted by the courts to include even indirect action, as, for example, the supplying of raw materials to the infringer *(mittelbare Patentverletzung)*. The infringement action is brought before ordinary courts.

REVOCATION PROCEEDINGS

which seek to declare a patent wholly or partially invalid is filed with the Federal Patent Court which was established as late as 1968. Appeal may be made to the Federal Supreme Court, on questions of both, law and facts, with the right to introduce new facts.

In general, decisions of the Patent Office are subject to an appeal to the Federal Patent Court, in particular by the applicant if his application is refused, or by a party whose objection to an application is refused by the Patent Office. A further appeal on questions of law to the Federal Supreme Court may be allowed from decisions of the Federal Patent Court.
Patents enjoy protection from year to year whether they are reduced to practice or not, as annual fees are paid for a maximum formerly of eighteen years, now of twenty after the filing date.

PATENT MARKINGS

are not required. The marking of "patent pending" or "applied for" is permissible at the earliest when the application has been laid open by the Patent Office. If such markings or assertions are made, the patent or the application must be identified upon demand of an interested party.

DESIGNS

Apart from patents, protection is possible under special statutes without examination for a new distinctive utility model and for creative commercial designs *(Gebrauchsmuster* and *Geschmacksmuster)*. A committee of the industry with the government participating must approve the commercial use of quality markings *(Gütezeichen)*.

TRADEMARKS *(Warenzeichen)* may be entered in a

Register

of the Patent Office *(Zeichenrolle)*. The trademark must be connected with an enterprise which is or will be engaged in the manufacture, processing or trading of goods. If the business of such enterprise is discontinued a third party may apply for cancellation of the trademark. Presently trademark protection is possible only for goods, but a government bill proposing the extension of trademark protection also to services is pending. A trademark may also be established by

mere use

and is protected if it has gained recognition in the trade. The Law does not define a trademark. It simply states that a trademark may be used to distinguish goods from those of another. A trademark must be distinctive. Mere letters, numbers or words of common language are not distinctive but may become so by extensive use and recognition in the trade ("4711"). A trademark may lose its protection if the owner does not prevent its general use. A registered trademark does not lose its validity simply by the fact that it is not used. A third party. however, may cause the cancellation of a trademark which has been registered for at least five years but which has not been used within the five years prior to the motion for cancellation. The

trademark application

is examined ex officio. Anyone who believes he possesses prior rights may file an objection. The objection based on an unused trademark which was registered for at least five years may be refused if the new applicant so requests. The granted trademark is published. Registration of trademarks is valid for ten years, effective from the date of application. It may be renewed for subsequent ten year periods. The registration of a trademark made on the basis of a foreign registration has a life of its own under the Madrid Union. Trademark infringements are dealt with by the ordinary courts.

Foreign Enterprises

which are not represented in Germany by a branch may apply for registration only if the country in which they operate grants reciprocity to German enterprises. Treaties have established reciprocity almost everywhere and have also done away with the requirement of first filing evidence for the protection of a foreign trademark abroad. It is also not required that the trademark goods be sold and shipped into Germany prior to registration. Foreign residents who do not have a place of business in Germany must appoint a resident attorney or patent attorney.

Transfer

The trademark may be transferred by assignment or by succession, but only together with the good-will of the enterprise or of that part of the enterprise in which the mark is used. The transfer must be registered if the successor wishes to assert his trademark rights. Trade associations may register trademarks for the use of their members *(Verbandszeichen)*.

Markings

While it is not required to indicate on the marked article that a trademark is registered or otherwise protected, it is advisable to do so. Foreign goods which are marked as being of German origin or which use a registered German trademark illegally may be seized and confiscated by the German customs authorities upon entry into Germany. If a foreign state requires that German goods must be marked as being of German origin or discriminates against German goods in customs clearance, the German Federal Minister of Finance may issue respective discriminatory regulations against the goods from such state and order the seizure and confiscation of foreign goods which do not comply with these regulations.

The exercise of the rights to a trade mark in a member state of the European Community whether it is based on a national application or on an application pursuant to the Madrid Union has come in conflict, for some time with the governing principle of free trade throughout the Community. The meaning of this "erosion of national trade mark rights" has been clarified to some extent by a recent decision of the German Federal Supreme Court following a requested binding decision of the European Court of Justice. It is accordingly compatible with the Rome Treaty that a firm objects to the import of goods of another firm if the trademark or other designation of the import can be confused with the first firm's trademark or other designation, provided, however, that there exist no agreements in restraint of trade nor any legal or economic dependence between the firms, and that their applicable industrial property rights have been established independently of each other. It is recommended that the firms employ additions to the designation of their goods in borderline cases. This seems to demand that the same limitations apply also to the proposed supranational

European trademark

a project, on which the negotiations have been resumed.

LICENSE

German law provides for the compulsory license of a patent or patent application if this is justified by the public interest – but not for antitrust reasons.

A compulsory license

is therefore granted if it is in the public interest. The claim for it must be made to the Federal Patent Court. The claimant must show that the patent owner refuses to allow the use of the patent upon application and that he has offered fair compensation and security to the owner therefor. The practical importance of this provision is negligible.

A voluntary offer

in writing to the Patent Office of a patent license to anybody at a reasonable royalty permits the owner of the patent to save one-half of the annual patent fees. This offer may not be withdrawn. It is registered and published.

An exclusive patent license may be registered. Trademarks cannot be licensed in the strict sense as they are considered to form an inseparable part of the good will of a business establishment. There is no statutory provision for the registration of trademark users. In practice, however, agreements for the use of trademarks are recognized as restrictive covenants of the trademark owner and enforceable as is any other obligatory contract.

Except for certain provisions of the cartel laws for the control of certain license clauses in restraint of trade, freedom of contract is not restricted in agreements to licence patents, patent applications and secret know-how. In interpreting rights and obligations of licensor and licensee which are not expressly regulated in the agreement, the courts make allowance for the fact that certain risks are inherent in such agreements, for example, unforseeable changes in technology or markets, or unexpected dependency upon older rights of third parties.

ART AND LITERATURE

The *Urheberrechtsgesetz* (1965) regulates the rights of authors of literary and artistic works in the broadest sense. Translations of books enjoy translator's rights of their own. The author's rights are inalienable but may be inherited. The Law provides in particular for rights of reproduction, distribution and exhibition in all forms, including radio and television, as well as licensing of such rights. The term of protection of the author's work has been extended to seventy years after the death of the author. A

102

register of authors *(Urheberrolle)* has been established at the Patent Office. The relations between author and publisher follow the *Verlagsgesetz* of 1901 as amended. Well organized is the collection of royalties for the exploitation of musical rights, for the making of copies of copyrighted works for commercial use and for the protection of other rights through private associations, formed or reorganized pursuant to a special Law (1965) and to certain requirements of German and European cartel law (GEMA case). Germany participates in the Bern Convention (1886) for the protection of Literature and Art, as amended in Paris, Rome and Brussels, and the Convention of Montevideo (1889), as well as the World Copyright Convention (1952) as amended and other multinational and bilateral treaties in this field including the production of television.

XIV. LABOR LAW AND SOCIAL INSURANCE

All law which regulates individual and collective relations between employers and employees or which otherwise applies to persons because of their dependence upon an employer is called labor law. Some of its provisions may be found in general statutes, such as the Civil and Commercial Codes, but the main body of labor law is contained in special statutes. Labor law is applied for administrative purposes by various governmental agencies. The

FEDERAL LABOR OFFICE *(Bundesanstalt für Arbeit)*

of which the local labor offices *(Arbeitsämter)* and the state labor offices *(Landesarbeitsämter)* form a part has a monopoly – with few exceptions – for the placement of personnel.

Private employment agencies are not permitted, not even for key personnel. But it is lawful to advertise openings for a specific position directly or indirectly by using the services of management consultants. The hiring out of personnel on a time basis is permitted under certain conditions which are laid down in a special statute.

All litigation in the labor field is administered by a special system of

LABOR COURTS *(Arbeitsgerichte)*

with elaborate procedural rules of their own. Employers and employees are equally represented as associate judges.

Labor law, being essentially for the protection of employees, is largely mandatory and if so it cannot be waived effectively by the parties in advance. The protection applies generally to every employee, however, as a rule not to the legal representatives of corporations i. e. the managing directors of the *GmbH* and the members of the board of management of the *AG*.

FOREIGN NATIONALS

German labor law applies as a rule to foreigners employed in the Federal Republic to the same extent as it does to German nationals. Stipulations that foreign law shall apply will be honored by German labor courts within certain limits if the employment relationship has sufficient connection with the territory to which the foreign law applies, i. e. if one party to the contract is a foreigner or if the contract is to be performed abroad. A German branch of a foreign corporation shall maintain the same institutions of German labor law as are prescribed for units of German enterprises: shop council *(Betriebsrat)*, economic committee *(Wirtschaftsausschuß)*. Free social mobility applies to nationals of the EEC member states. Other foreign nationals are admitted if they can show satisfactory openings. If such foreign nationals are employed in Germany with foreign or domestic enterprises, working permits must be obtained prior to the commencement of the employment unless the employee qualifies as an executive, as an officer of the company *(Vorstand (AG), Geschäftsführer (GmbH)* or *Prokurist)*. In addition to the working permit every such foreign national must obtain a residence permit, usually in the form of a visa, if he intends to take up employment in the Federal Republic or to stay there for more than three months. The permit will be granted for a specific period of time. The follows the general law of contract, but there are numerous mandatory rules affording special protection for employees. Apart from special protection of disabled persons, expectant mothers, minors etc. there exist general statutory regulations of maximum working hours, working conditions, legal holidays, vacation leave, vocational training, but none for minimum salaries or wages. Several statutes regulate the

termination of employment.

The minimum period required for notice of termination varies with wage earners and salaried employees, age and seniority, and certain specific circumstances, such as pregnancy, disability, etc.

Salaried employees must receive six weeks notice prior to the end of a calendar quarter. This period, however, may be shortened in the contract of employment to the minimum of one month, becoming effective at the end of a calendar month. The period of notice is extended to three months after five years of employment, to four months after eight years, to five months after ten years and to six months after twelve years of employment. In all these cases the period of notice terminates at the end of the next following calendar quarter and may not be reduced in advance.

The period of notice for wage earners is normally two weeks. It is extended to one month per the end of a month after five years of service, to two months per the end of a month after ten years and to three months per the end of a calender quarter after twenty years of service. The notice period may be shortened or extended by collective labor agreements.

Furthermore, according to the *Kündigungsschutzgesetz*, a salaried employee or a wage earner who has been employed by the same enterprise for more than six months cannot be discharged by enterprises which employ regularly more than five persons, if the discharge is "socially unjustified". A discharge is socially justified primarily for reasons relating to the person or conduct of the employee; or for urgent business reasons if the employee cannot be transferred to another suitable occupation in the firm. In the latter case the employer must show that he has considered the social aspects in selecting the employee concerned. Legal action by the employee must be brought within three weeks after the receipt of the notice of termination. Dismissal without observance of a period of notice is permitted for cause only. Cause will be held to exist if the continuation of the employment appears to be intolerable for the employer, all circumstances considered; a dismissal for cause is valid, however, only if notice is given within two weeks after the reasons giving rise to the dismissal have become known to the employer. In all cases of a dismissal the shop council *(Betriebsrat)* must be heard in advance. Failure to comply with this requirement invalidates the dismissal. Within certain limits employment for a trial period or for a predetermined period of time is possible.

Mass dismissals

in enterprises with more than 20 employees are subject to prior notification of the local labor office in order to become effective. The office must be notified in writing together with the shop council's opinion within statutory terms which vary according to the number of dismissals relative to the enterprise's size. Subsequent to notification, a one-month period will commence during which no dismissal is effective .unless specifically approved by the state labor office. The state labor office may shorten or extend the said period. In the case of cut-backs or shut-downs certain procedures must be followed in order to avoid hardship to the employees.

NON-COMPETITION CLAUSE

During the time of employment the obligation of the employee to refrain from any competitive activity follows from the general loyalty he owes to his employer. This is established by statute for clerical personnel in a commercial enterprise, but is held to apply also to other employees.The principle of loyalty applies also to pensioners of the enterprise. For a specified period after termination of the employment, which in no event may exceed two years, a competitive activity of the employee can be restricted through agreement in advance. Such agreement must be in writing with a signed copy to the employee and is subject to a number of limitations and conditions, in particular the employee must be paid during the non-competition period at least half of his contractual remuneration as compensation. Any such agreement must be justified by the business interests of the employer and must be free of undue restrictions on the employee. If it is not, the clause is void.

EMPLOYEE INVENTIONS

are regulated in detail by the *Gesetz über Arbeitnehmererfindungen*. The provisions protecting the employee may not be waived in advance. The employee must report his inventions to the employer who may claim them for his exclusive or nonexclusive use in return for a reasonable compensation. Compensation rules to determine reasonable fees have been worked out by the Federal Minister of Labor. They are not binding. Many major enterprises have developed a remuneration system of their own. Income from inventions is granted a tax preference – this privilege is not limited to employee inventors.

CO-DETERMINATION

Employees enjoy the statutory right of cooperation or co-determination with the management of their enterprise in certain matters which affect their social or economic welfare and security. The basic statute is the *Betriebsverfassungsgesetz* (Shop Constitution Law). It provides for the institution of the

Betriebsrat (Shop Council)

as the official representation of the employees towards company management. Not included in such representation are

leitende Angestellte (managing employees),

a term which the Law attempts to define in some detail. Shop councils may be formed in enterprises or separate enterprise units employing regularly at least five persons; management is under no obligation to initiate the formation of a shop council. The powers and functions of the shop council relate to social, personnel and economic matters. In the area of

social matters

the right of participation and co-determination of the council is most clear-cut and strongest. The shop council has a right of co-determination, for example, with respect to the following matters: fixing of the beginning and end of the daily working and rest hours; temporary reductions or extensions of normal working hours; time, place and manner of the payment of employment compensation; vacation planning; introduction and use of technical performance and conduct of control devices; social facilities; and compensation principles and methods. These matters require agreement between management and the council. In

personnel matters

the participation rights of the shop council cover both general and individual personnel matters.

The employer must inform the shop council comprehensively on personnel planning, in particular on the present and future personnel requirements and the personnel measures and provisions for career development arising therefrom, and must consult with the shop council on such matters. The council may require that vacant positions are advertised within the enterprise. Personnel questionnaires and principles of evaluation are subject to shop council approval; the same applies to selection guidelines with respect to employment, transfers, reclassifications and dismissals.

In shops employing more than twenty persons the employer shall advise the shop council prior to each new employment, classification, reclassification and transfer. These measures are subject to the shop council's approval. The council may, however, only refuse to grant its approval for certain limited reasons specified in the Law. Particular provisions regulate the shop council's co-determination with respect to dismissals. The council must be consulted prior to each notice of dismissal; a notice given without prior consultation is void. With respect to

economic matters

the employer must inform the shop council comprehensively and consult with the council on contemplated shop modifications which might result in substantial disadvantages for the personnel. Such modifications include cut-backs and shut-downs, relocations, mergers, fundamental changes in the organization, purpose, and installations of the enterprise, and the introduction of fundamentally new working methods or manufacturing processes.
The employer and the shop council shall establish a compromise between the conflicting interests *(Interessenausgleich)*, on the contemplated shop modification and an agreement on the compensation for the mitigation of the economic disadvantages which the employees will suffer as a consequence of the contemplated shop modification *(Sozialplan* – social plan).
In enterprises with more than 100 employees, an economic committee *(Wirtschaftsausschuß)* must be formed whose members are appointed by the shop council and may include managing employees. The rights of the economic committee are limited to rights of information and consultation on the economic affairs of the enterprise.
The *Betriebsverfassungsgesetz* provides for many instances where a binding decision shall be made by an

Einigungsstelle (Conciliation Board)

when no agreement can be reached between the employer and the shop council. The conciliation board comprises an equal number of members to be appointed by the employer and the shop council and an impartial chairman. The conciliation board is formed ad hoc for the purpose of settling a particular dispute, but a permanent conciliation board may be established by shop agreement. The decisions of the conciliation board are appealable to the labor court only on very limited grounds.

109

A further right of co-determination is vested in the employees through their

participation in boards

of supervision *(Aufsichtsrat)* of corporations. In all *AGs* and in *GmbHs* employing more than 500 persons labor representatives participate with one third, and in corporations employing more than 2000 persons labor representatives participate with one half in the supervisory board. The labor representatives participate therefore via their membership in the supervisory board in *AGs* and large *GmbHs* in the appointment of the corporations's chief executives, the *Geschäftsführer* of the *GmbH* and the *Vorstand* of the *AG*.

COLLECTIVE LABOR AGREEMENTS

Labor agreements through collective bargaining are made as a rule between the employers' association on the one side and unions or other qualified labor associations on the other in accordance with the applicable statute *(Tarifvertragsgesetz)*. They are as a rule regional agreements by trades. There are no closed or union shops, nor featherbedding agreements. The labor agreements are usually confined to the special conditions of a particular trade, mainly to wages and working time, whereas general labor law adequately protects employees in all other respects. On special application the agreements may be given the force of law by the competent state authority, thus applying also to employers and employees who are not parties or members of parties to the agreement. But even if no such decision has been made, the conditions of the collective labor agreements usually are applied to all employees of the enterprise.

SHOP AGREEMENTS *(Betriebsvereinbarungen)*

are made between the individual employer and the shop council representing the employees. These agreements must be in writing. They may not cover matters which are the subject of regional collective bargaining agreements.

SOCIAL INSURANCE, PENSIONS

Social insurance covers sickness, workmen's compensation, unemployment insurance and pensions. Workmen's compensation insurance is borne exclusivly by the employer. Pension, sickness and unemployment insurance are on a contributory basis, with the employer and employee each contributing one half of the premium; in addition, the government grants subsidies to pensioners and for maternity benefits. It pays the total costs of family allowances. Pension and unemployment insurance are now obligatory for all employees, including legal representatives and officers of corporations with the exception of members of the board of management of the *Aktiengesellschaft*. Sickness insurance is obligatory only for employees up to a specified amount of income.
Voluntary

PENSION GRANTS

by the employer are quite common. They are secured by mandatory law. The pension rights become vested rights when the employee has completed his 35th year of life and the grant has been in effect for 10 years or for only 3 years in case of 12 years of service. The pensions are protected against the insolvency of the employer by a pension insurance scheme. The employer must review every 3 years whether or not the pension should be equitably adjusted, particularly to account for increases in living costs.

FOREIGN NATIONALS

employed in Germany are in principle also covered by the German social insurance system. However, in addition to the social insurance regulations of the EEC, social insurance conventions have been entered into between the Federal Republic and a number of other countries concerning the social insurance position of foreigners taking up employment in Germany. The recently concluded convention between Germany and the United States is not yet in effect. Absent special regulation in an applicable convention, foreign nationals sent to work in Germany for any specified period of time, but remaining in the employ of their foreign employer, are exempt from German social insurance.

XV. TAXATION

The main types of German taxes of interest to business are the following:

Transfer Taxes (*Verkehrsteuern*)

Turnover Tax (*Umsatzsteuer*)
Capital Investment Tax
(*Kapitalverkehrsteuer* or *Gesellschaftssteuer*)
Stock Exchange Turnover Tax (*Börsenumsatzsteuer*)
Bills of Exchange Tax (*Wechselsteuer*)
Real Estate Acquisition Tax (*Grunderwerbsteuer*)

Income Taxes (*Einkommensteuern*)

Corporation Income Tax (*Körperschaftsteuer*)
Personal Income Tax (*Einkommensteuer*)
Trade Income Tax (*Gewerbeertragssteuer*)

and

Net Worth Tax (*Vermögensteuer*).

All of these taxes are based on federal statutes but are administered by the states except that the Real Estate Acquisition Tax is amended by statutes of the states, and that the municipalities codetermine the trade tax rate and administer it to some extent themselves. Detailed implementing regulations (*Steuerrichtlinien*) are issued from time to time by the federal government; they are binding for the administration but not for the courts.

The tax courts, to which all decisions of the tax authorities can be appealed, apply a very strict and formal interpretation of the statutes, when dealing with transfer taxes, while in the field of income taxes the interpretation is not as formal. Tax authorities and tax courts will give more weight to substance than to form.

The true parties and the true business purpose of the transaction form the basis of taxation.

These principles are to some extent set forth in the Fiscal Code *(Abgabenordnung: AO)* which was revised effective as of on January 1, 1977. The hope that the revised code would contain a general rule requiring the tax authorities to give binding rulings on how they would treat a specific situation in terms of taxation has not been fulfilled. Only on the basis of a tax audit will the tax authorities give a written ruling which is binding if the facts later turn out to be such as stated in the ruling. The tax authorities will still occasionally give advance rulings which are not legally binding but are factually helpful.

Tax returns must, as a rule, be filed annually, except in case of non-recurring taxes, which are to be reported when the facts on which they are based occur.

The tax returns are subject to review. A tax assessment will only be made if the return is found to be incorrect. The assessment period has been reduced to four years, except in case of gross negligence when the period is five years and in case of fraud when the period is ten years. The period during which the tax may be collected is five years from the end of the year in which the return has been filed or the assessment become final.

The taxpayer prepays his income tax or corporation income tax in four quarterly instalments. The prepayments are based on the tax returns filed for the preceding year. Prepayments may upon request or ex officio, be reduced or increased if the current income differs substantially from that shown in the last tax return.

Certain taxes are withheld at source, in particular the wage tax in the case of income from employment and the capital yields tax in the case of dividend income.

Turnover Tax
(Added Value Tax, *Umsatzsteuer, Mehrwertsteuer*)

Based on the provisions of the Rome Treaty contemplating a harmonization of the indirect tax systems of the member states and on recommendation of the Common Market authorities, Germany introduced an Added Value Turnover Tax (*Mehr-*

wertsteuer) Law, as of January 1, 1968, which replaced the former, cumulative all-stage Turnover Tax Law.

The tax is levied on the amounts received for goods delivered and services rendered within Germany.

For the purpose of determining whether a delivery is made within Germany, it is not decisive whether the contract is signed in Germany, or whether the invoice is issued or payment is received in Germany. The decisive factor is only where delivery actually takes place or is deemed to take place. If the goods are to be shipped to the customer either by the seller himself or by a common carrier, delivery is deemed to be made where the shipment begins or where the merchandise is handed over to the carrier. This means that imported goods are not subject to the general turnover tax. They are, however, subject to an import turnover tax (*Einfuhrumsatzsteuer*), which follows the rules of customs law, so that imported goods are burdened with the same tax as domestic goods.

The term "services" covers, for turnover tax purposes, a very wide range of activities. It includes leasing of machinery within Germany, licensing of German patents and trademarks, rendering of professional services, or providing manpower or know-how. However, if the know-how is made available from abroad, for instance by sending drawings, descriptions, specifications by mail and training personnel in a foreign plant, the compensation received therefor is not subject to turnover tax, as this constitutes a service rendered outside of Germany.

Goods exported from Germany are exempt from turnover tax. In addition, certain services rendered to foreign principals, or services which are to be utilized outside of Germany – such as the engineering work for foreign plants, the furnishing of know-how to be utilized outside of Germany, or the acting as sales agent for foreign principals – are likewise exempt.

The added value turnover tax is assessed on the net price paid for the goods sold or the services rendered. The tax itself must be shown separately in the invoice to qualify as a deductible pre-tax. The tax rate as of January 1, 1978 is generally 12 per cent, but is reduced to 6 per cent for foodstuffs, books, printed matter and certain professional services.

114

Any turnover tax a customer has paid to his supplier can be deducted by him from his own monthly turnover tax liability incurred on account of his own sales or services as a so-called pre-tax. If the deductible pre-tax amount is higher than the customer's own turnover tax liability he can claim a refund from the tax office. By this method the law achieves the result that only the value added at each stage is taxed and that the final tax burden is shifted to the ultimate consumer. This can be illustrated by the following example:

Producer A sells at a price of 100 plus 12 turnover tax to Manufacturer B who in turn sells at a price of 120 plus 14.40 turnover tax to Dealer C who sells at 150 plus 18 to the ultimate consumer. A pays to the tax office the amount of 12 billed to B; B pays to the tax office 2.40 (14.40 minus 12); C pays to the tax office 3.60 (18.00 minus 14.40). The total amount paid to the tax office is 18, namely the amount charged to the ultimate consumer by C.

The system, as a rule, does not work to the disadvantage of foreigners, as indicated in the following example:

Foreign company A has licensed German patents to its German licensee B for a lump sum royalty of 100 plus 12 turnover tax. A had retained the German advertising agency C to advertise for the patented product. C has charged A 50 plus 6 turnover tax. A pays as turnover tax the 12 received from its licensee minus the 6 billed to him by the advertising agency. A foreigner, therefor, only suffers a disadvantage under the added value tax law when services are rendered to him within Germany whereby he incurs a turnover tax while he himself has no German turnover tax liability against which he could credit the turnover tax billed to him. Such situations arise primarily when foreign manufacturers supply their German customer from abroad and therefor incur no German turnover tax liability but have sought to develop their German sales by an advertising campaign in Germany for which the advertising agency has billed them for the German turnover tax in addition to the costs. The tax in this situation is thus "lost". If these amounts are significant, it is, therefor, preferable, for the foreign manufacturer to deliver from stock in Germany, and thereby to incur German turnover tax liability against which the turnover tax billed to him can be credited. No additional tax burden is thereby created.

Deliveries of goods from West Berlin into West Germany are privileged. The West Berlin supplier may deduct, as the case may, be between 4.5 per cent and 6 per cent of the selling price from his turnover tax liability, while the West German customer is entitled to a deduction of 4.2 per cent.

Capital Investment Tax (*Kapitalverkehrsteuer*)

is levied on transactions which strengthen the capital position of German corporations. It is payable, in particular, upon the formation of a German corporation or upon a capital increase by the corporation. But it applies also to:

other contributions by a shareholder of a German corporation made by virtue of an obligation created in the articles of association;

voluntary contributions made by a shareholder of a German corporation which increase the value of the shares owned, such as forgiving of claims, selling goods to the company below their value, purchasing goods from the company in excess of their market price;

the assumption of losses of a subsidiary corporation by virtue of a profit and loss pooling agreement;

moving the management or the domicile of a non-resident corporation into Germany, if the foreign corporation thereby becomes a German corporation, unless the non-resident corporation was, prior to such move, for capital investment tax purposes, treated as a corporation in a member state of the Common Market;

contributions made by a non-resident corporation to the fixed assets and working capital of its German permanent establishment, irrespective of whether the same is registered as a branch in the Commercial Register, except when the non-resident corporation has its management or its domicile in a member state of the Common Market.

The tax rate is 1 per cent.

The basis for the tax assessment is the amount of the capital invested but at least the value of the shares. When the investment is made to rehabilitate a German company, the tax rate is under certain conditions reduced to one half of the regular rate. The tax is assessed against the German corporation in which the investment is made. However, the shareholder making the investment is also liable for the payment of the tax.

Initial or subsequent contributions by the limited partners of a limited partnership in which the general partner is a corporation *(GmbH & Co KG)* are taxed as if made to a corporation. The tax is also levied when the general partner is not a corporation but again a *GmbH & Co KG*, the so-called two-tier limited partnership. The Capital Investment Tax constitutes a deductible expense except to the extent it can be covered out of a premium paid. Since January 1, 1972 the tax is no longer levied on shareholder loans.

Stock Exchange Turnover Tax
(Börsenumsatzsteuer)

Contracts for the acquisition of securities for a consideration, such as shares in a domestic or foreign corporation, warrants, share certificates, shares in mutual funds, bonds, debentures, regardless of where issued, (except for the first acquisition which is covered by the capital investment tax), are subject to the tax when the transaction takes place within Germany, or, if outside of Germany, when at least one party to the transaction is a German resident.

Transactions effected by letter, cable, telephone or telex between a place in Germany and a place abroad are deemed to be concluded abroad.

Transactions strictly between banks, dealers, brokers or mutual funds, irrespective of nationality or residence, are exempt from the tax, unless *GmbH* shares are involved. Redemptions by mutual funds are likewise tax exempt.

The tax rate varies between 0.1 per cent and 0.25 per cent. The rate is reduced by one-half if the agreement is entered into abroad and only one party is a German resident.

Bills of Exchange Tax (*Wechselsteuer*)

Bills of exchange and negotiable promissory notes issued in Germany or issued abroad but acquired in Germany are subject to a 0.15 per cent stamp tax. The tax is reduced by one-half for bills drawn in Germany on a foreign drawee and payable abroad, and for bills drawn abroad on a domestic drawee and payable in Germany.

Real Estate Acquisition Tax (*Grunderwerbsteuer*)

applies under broad definitions, to all transactions with the purpose or effect of transferring title to German real estate and buildings and hereditary building rights (*Erbbaurecht*). The tax is also assessed when all of the shares of a German or foreign corporation which owns real estate in Germany are acquired, or when a shareholder owning less than all of the shares of such a company subsequently acquires the balance of the shares. In line with the formal interpretation of transfer tax laws the Federal Fiscal Court has ruled that the tax does not become due in this event when as little as a fraction of one per cent of the shares of the company is still held by a genuine third party. However, some state statutes prescribe that the acquisition of all shares is deemed to be accomplished when only 95 or 98 per cent have been acquired.

The acquisition of a participation in a partnership owning real estate does not lead to the assessment of the tax. The tax will only become due at the dissolution of the partnership when one partner acquires the real estate, but in this event, provided he has been a partner for at least five years, the tax is only assessed on the balance not previously owned by the partner. The tax becomes further due when all shares of a partnership are united in one hand or in the hands of dominating and dependent enterprises.

The tax rate is usually 7 per cent and is assessed on the consideration given for the transfer. When no consideration is given or none can be ascertained, or, in particular, when all of the shares of a company holding German real estate are acquired, the basis for the assessment is the tax value of the real

estate which is as a rule lower than the market value. Whenever real estate is transferred to a German corporation as a contribution in kind, the tax is reduced to 6 per cent of the consideration given.
Transferor and transferee are jointly and severally liable for the tax. In case all shares of a corporation or partnership are united in the hands of one person only such person is liable for the payment of the tax. The tax constitutes part of the acquisition costs of the real estate or of the shares.

INCOME TAXES

Corporation Income Tax (*Körperschaftsteuer*)

The world wide income of resident corporations, i. e. corporations having either their management or their domicile in Germany is subject to this tax. However, this principle is limited to a great extent by the numerous conventions for the avoidance of double taxation concluded by Germany.
The income of partnerships is not subject to the Corporation Income Tax, it is directly taxed with the partners. If the partners are corporations, corporation income tax is assessed against them; if the partners are individuals, personal income tax is assessed.
Non-resident corporations are subject to German corporation income tax on certain types of income derived from German sources, in particular when they maintain a permanent establishment within Germany.
The taxable income of a corporation is taken from a balance sheet established for .fiscal purposes and constitutes the difference between the net worth of the corporation at the end of the fiscal year and the net worth at the end of the preceding fiscal year, subject to some adjustments, in particular for capital paid in or withdrawn and for hidden distributions of profit.
On January 1, 1977 the German Corporation Income Tax Law has undergone a fundamental change. The system of taxing the corporation's profit at two levels, at the level of the corporation and at the level of the shareholder, has been abolished. It has been replaced by an imputation system. The profit is only taxed

once. This is accomplished by allowing the shareholder, if he is a resident tax-payer, a full credit for the income tax paid by the corporation.

The determination of taxable income and deductible business expenses under fiscal accounting principles does not vary greatly from those practiced in the United States.

Depreciation (*Abschreibung*)

Property, plant and equipment are depreciated over the expected lifetime of the individual asset. The Federal Minister of Finance publishes from time to time lists of approved depreciation rates which are not mandatory, but the burden of proof in justifying deviation therefrom is placed, for all practical purposes, on the taxpayer. Land cannot be depreciated. As a rule, the choice is between the straight line or the declining balance method, but in the latter case the annual depreciation rate may not exceed 25 per cent. It is possible to change over from the declining balance method to the straight line method but not vice versa. With respect to buildings, only the straight line method is as a rule permissible.

Special more favourable depreciation rates apply to property, plant and equipment used either exclusively or primarily for research or development purposes.

Special more favourable depreciation rates also apply to property situated in West-Berlin and certain border areas or in other areas of Germany officially designated as being industrially underdeveloped.

Items having a minor value, presently of not more than DM 800,–, can be fully written off in the year of acquisition.

Inventory (*Vorräte*)

is to be valued at the lower of cost or market value. With respect to certain inventory items which are subject to substantial price fluctuation, a tax-free reserve may be established and be maintained for a maximum period of six years. Further, the cost of certain raw material considered to be of importance for the German economy may be depreciated by up to 20 per cent per annum.

Capital Gains (*Veräußerungsgewinne*)

For corporations, capital gains constitute ordinary business income which is not subject to any preferred tax rate. However, under certain conditions gains resulting from the sale of capital assets such as land, buildings, assets having an expected lifetime of at least twenty-five years, ships and shares in domestic or foreign corporations are tax-free if reinvested in certain other capital assets within two years, in some cases within four years, following the fiscal year of disposal. During this period the gain can be carried as a tax-free reserve. If not utilized during this period it must be dissolved and constitutes ordinary taxable income, but otherwise it permits a tax-free exchange of assets.

Hidden Profit Distribution
(*Constructive Dividend; Verdeckte Gewinnausschüttung*)

A corporation's profits may not be reduced by any manipulated transaction between the corporation, its shareholders and other affiliated companies. All transactions between the corporation and its shareholders must pass the "arm's-lenght" test, i. e. the terms must be the same as those agreed upon with independent third parties. Provided this is the case, management fees, interest, or royalties paid to a shareholder constitute deductible business expenses. If not, the total expense or the excess will be disallowed, considered as a hidden profit distribution and imputed as a profit to the corporation.

Rehabilitation Gains (*Sanierungsgewinne*)

A gain realized by a reduction of the corporation's capital and the normally simultaneous increase of capital does not affect its income. The same applies when for rehabilitation purposes debts of a corporation are forgiven. The gain realized thereby need not be applied against the corporation's loss carry-forward. Any payments later made by the corporation on the forgiven debt do not qualify as a business expense, because expenses connected with non-taxable income, such as the rehabilitation gain, do not qualify for a deduction.

Loss Carry Forward (*Verlustvortrag*) – Loss Carry Back (*Verlustrücktrag*)

Losses of up to DM 5 million are to be carried back for one year. Losses that cannot be offset against the taxable income of the immediately preceding year are to be carried forward for five subsequent years. The loss carried back is credited against the prior year's taxable income that has suffered tax at the full 56 per cent rate of tax. The loss carry forward or loss carry back is only available to the company which has incurred the loss. In a merger, the loss carry forward of the merging company is, therefor, not available to the surviving company. Furthermore, the loss carry forward is not available if the company has totally changed its character, as it is then no longer considered to be identical with the one that incurred the loss. Acquisitions of corporate shells, where the only asset is a loss carry forward, are, therefor, not attractive.

German corporations and partnerships may set up a tax-free reserve in the amount of the start-up losses of their foreign subsidiaries provided the following conditions are met: the interest in the foreign subsidiary must have been acquired after January 1, 1969; the interest must amount to at least 50 per cent of the share capital (in case the subsidiary is domiciled in a less developed country, a 25 per cent interest is sufficient); the foreign subsidiary must be an actual trading or producing company. Holding companies, leasing companies or patent licensing companies do not qualify. The tax-free reserve is to be dissolved within five years at the latest, or earlier when the taxpayer sells his interest in the foreign subsidiary.

Foreign Tax Credit

To the extent that the foreign income of a corporation is not exempt from German tax by virtue of a tax convention, the corporation is entitled to claim a credit for foreign income tax paid, but only up to the amount of the corresponding German tax, which is allocable to the income from the respective foreign

122

country ("per country limitation"). Furthermore an indirect tax credit is available for profit distributions by foreign controlled subsidiaries. On the other hand the income of foreign controlled subsidiaries in taxhaven countries not engaged in active business operations will be attributed to their German shareholders.

Corporation Income Tax Rates

The split corporation income tax rate structure introduced in 1959 to encourage dividend distributions and to promote the capital market has been retained when in 1977 the German Corporation Income Tax Law underwent a fundamental change. The distributed profit is still favoured by a lower tax, namely by a rate of 36 per cent versus a rate of 56 per cent on retained profits. The rate of 56 per cent is only an initial rate, which is reduced to 36 per cent on distribution regardless when such distribution takes place. On the other hand, when the income had at first not been subject to any tax or a lower tax than 36 per cent, the 36 per cent tax rate is now applied at the time of distribution.

The maximum dividend out of a taxable profit of DM 100,– is, therefore, DM 64,–. At the shareholder level the cash dividend received will be grossed up to DM 100,– by the credit for the DM 36,– tax paid by the corporation.

The shareholder will be entitled to claim the DM 36,– as a full credit against his own personal income tax. If his income tax rate should be 56 per cent, which is the highest tax rate for individuals, the DM 100,– profit of the corporation will then effectively have been taxed at the rate of 56 per cent without any double taxation. If the individual's tax rate should be less than 36 per cent, the individual is entitled to claim a refund from the tax office for the excess amount. The tax credit is, however, only available to shareholders, who are subject to general German tax jurisdiction, and therefor not to foreign shareholders. They cannot gross up and benefit from the tax credit. Foreign shareholders are only in two exceptional cases entitled to claim a credit for the income tax paid by the German corporation, namely when a distribution of profits is concerned which have arisen prior to the change of the tax system, i. e. before January 1, 1977, or when taxfree foreign income of the German corporation is distributed. The German withholding tax on dividends remains to be paid in these cases. The 1977 tax reform has, therefore, considerably increased the German tax burden for foreign shareholders.

In order to accomplish its aim of taxing the corporation's profit only once, the statute divides the corporation's income into three classes:

i)   income which has been subject to unreduced corporation tax, i. e. 56 per cent

ii) income which has been subject to reduced corporation income tax, i. e. 36 per cent

iii) income which has not been subject to corporation income tax, i. e. taxfree income

Income which has been subject to rates lower than 36 per cent is prorated to classes ii) and iii); income which has been subject to rates between 56 and 36 per cent is prorated to classes i) and ii). Profit distributions are deemed to be made from that class of income which has borne the highest tax burden.

Corporations which are resident in Berlin benefit from certain reductions.

Complete Relief for Distributed Profits

In order to ensure that all profit taxed at the level of the corporation is ultimately taxed only at the rate applicable to the resident shareholder, the tax credit is not limited to dividends paid in the ordinary course, but it is also available to distributions made on the liquidation of a corporation or to gains realized in connection with reorganization transactions. There is no time limit on the crediting of the tax paid at the level of the corporation.

Stock Dividends *(Schütt aus hol zurück)*

German corporations may increase their share capital by transferring surplus reserves to capital. The new shares created

124

thereby can be distributed free of income tax to the shareholders. However, the surplus from 1977 and the following years' earnings transferred to reserves have in this event suffered the full 56 per cent tax rate applicable to retained earnings.

The term stock dividend is often employed inappropriately to describe the procedure when a German corporation distributes its profits on the basis of a proper shareholders' resolution (thus qualifying for the lower tax rate on distributed earnings) and when immediately thereafter the shareholder reinvests the net amount received by subscribing to new shares of the German corporation. This method is advantageous for the resident shareholder who receives a full credit for the corporation income tax paid by the company, and also for the non-resident shareholder if he benefits from a reduced withholding tax on dividends under a tax convention and when, therefore, the total of the withholding tax and the reduced corporation income tax is less than the amount of tax which the subsidiary would have to pay if it merely retained the earnings. It may also lead to more advantageous tax treatment in the country of the recipient.

Capital Yields Tax *(Kapitalertragsteuer)*

The profits distributed as dividends are taxed by a capital yields tax at the rate of 25 per cent, which is withheld at source. It is not an additional tax but qualifies as a full tax credit against the recipient's income tax if the recipient is a resident taxpayer. Only with respect to foreign dividend recipients who are not otherwise subject to German taxation, does it constitute an actual tax burden, but this may be mitigated under one of the many tax conventions concluded by Germany and, in addition, may be offset by a tax credit in the recipient's home country.

The capital yields tax rate is 33.33 per cent of the amount paid when the tax is not to be borne by the recipient of the dividend but by the distributing corporation, which is assumed in the case of hidden profit distributions.

125

Taxation of Hidden Profit Distributions
(Constructive Dividend – *Verdeckte Gewinnausschüttung*)

When at a tax audit the tax authorities find that a transaction between the shareholder and the corporation does not pass the arm's length test, e. g. when royalties or management fees are considered as excessive, the excess amount will be imputed to the corporation's profit and be considered as profit distribution or a constructive dividend. Such profit will in principle be taxed at the same rate as a profit distributed in accordance with a proper shareholders' resolution, namely at the rate of 36 per cent, and the tax will be available as a credit against the resident taxpayer's own tax liability. However, this presupposes that the corporation having made the hidden profit distribution has not always made a full distribution of all of its profit. If it has and accordingly has no retained earnings, the tax rate on a hidden profit distribution rises in the year of distribution to 112,25 per cent, as compared to the normal 36 per cent. However, if a longer period is considered, the tax rate on hidden profit distributions is the same as on open profit distributions. The higher tax rate with which hidden profit distributions are punished poses therefore only a liquidity problem.

Intercorporate Dividends
(Affiliation Privilege *Schachtelprivileg*)

Under the new imputation tax system the former affiliation privilege, which had served to avoid taxing the same profit, both at the level of the subsidiary and of the parent corporation, is no longer required. Distributions from a German subsidiary to a German parent corporation carry a credit of 36 per cent for the tax paid by the subsidiary. The distribution and the gross up are included in full in the income of the parent corporation and taxed at the rate of 56 per cent. Thus the income at the corporate level remains subject to the rate of 56 per cent until the profit is distributed to the ultimate individual shareholders. At that time the reduction in corporate tax coupled with the full crediting of the remaining 36 per cent of tax completely eliminates taxation at the corporate level. The minimum holding of 25 per cent in the subsidiary for a full year is therefore no longer relevant as far as the corporation income tax is concerned. It is still a requirement for tax relief for the net worth tax and the trade tax on income and capital.

Integrated Companies *(Organschaft)*

When a German corporation, the subsidiary, from the beginning of its fiscal year has been wholly integrated, financially, economically, and administratively into another German corporation or into a German partnership or into the German branch of a foreign corporation, and when a written profit and loss pooling agreement *(Ergebnisabführungsvertrag)* has been concluded for at least five years, the profit of the subsidiary company is not distributed as a dividend, but accrues directly to the parent company and, consequently, is only taxed with the parent company. By the same token, any losses incurred by the subsidiary are directly charged against the taxable income of the parent company. This relationship is commonly called an *Organschaft*. It has lost some of its former attraction because under the new corporation income tax law the parent company can automatically take a full credit for the corporation income tax paid by the subsidiary, but *Organschaft* is still of importance for taking over losses of a subsidiary.

Sale of an interest in a Domestic Corporation by a Nonresident Shareholder to a Resident Shareholder

The law provides in this situation for a rather complex procedure to ensure that the non-resident shareholder does not by the sale achieve the same result as if he had been eligible for a credit for the 36 per cent income tax paid by the domestic corporation on profit distributions. The law treats in this case any amount paid by the purchaser in excess of the stated capital of the domestic corporation, be it as compensation for retained earnings or for hidden reserves or for good will, as a

127

contribution of the purchaser to the capital of the domestic corporation. Insofar as the domestic corporation has retained earnings, the tax burden suffered by them becomes final. Insofar as the purchase price exceeds stated capital and retained earnings, i. e. insofar as it reflects hidden reserves or good will, any profit subsequently earned by the domestic corporation is regardless of distribution taxed at the rate of 56 per cent applicable to retained earnings until the amount of after tax profits equals the excess of the purchase price over stated capital and retained earnings. Whenever such retained earnings or after tax profits are distributed to the resident purchaser such distribution does not result in a reduction of the corporation income tax rate to 36 per cent and does not entitle the resident shareholder to a 36 per cent tax credit, however, such distribution is not taxed in the hands of the resident purchaser either since it is considered a repayment of a contribution to capital which reduces the book value of the investment.

The above rules only apply if the non-resident shareholder held during the last five years preceding the sale an interest of more than 25 per cent of the capital of the domestic corporation or an interest in a nominal amount of at least *DM* 1 million.

The same rules apply when the selling shareholder is not a non-resident shareholder but for other reasons not subject to general German income tax liability, such as for instance a tax exempt German corporation under public law.

The above rules do not apply when the non-resident shareholder sells the interest in the domestic corporation to another non-resident, or when the consideration paid is less than DM 100 000,–.

The above rules are in many cases likely to temporarily subject a resident purchaser to a higher tax burden than a non-resident purchaser. This will affect the purchase price which the non-resident shareholder may be able to realize from a sale of his interest in the domestic corporation.

There are good chances that the effect of the above rules can be avoided if the domestic corporation subsequent to the purchase is merged into the resident purchaser, however such merger requires share ownership of at least 90 per cent.

128

Merger (Umwandlung)

Already the 1969 merger tax law (Umwandlungssteuergesetz) had removed many of the hitherto existing tax disadvantages which had often barred mergers or other reorganizations within a corporate group. In accordance with the 1977 tax reform, which seeks to eliminate the double taxation of dividends by crediting the shareholders with the income tax paid by the corporation, the merger tax law has now been amended. The surviving company may continue the book values of the merged corporation. Only at the time when the undisclosed reserves of the merged corporation result in dividend payments of the surviving corporation will they become subject to income tax, and this tax paid by the surviving corporation is available as a full credit against the income tax liability of the resident shareholders of the surviving corporation. If, on the other hand, the merger should result in a loss to the surviving corporation, such loss will not be recognized for tax purposes. Likewise, any loss carry-forward of the merged corporation cannot be taken over, it is "lost" as a result of the merger.

The Law further permits other tax free mergers, namely the transfer of certain assets against shares. Qualifying assets are: a business unit (Betrieb), a separate division of a business unit (Teilbetrieb), a participation in a partnership or all of the shares of a corporation. The receiving corporation may also be a new corporation specifically formed for that purpose. It is not necessary for the transferor to acquire a substantial interest in the receiving corporation. The receiving corporation has the option of continuing the book values of the acquired assets or of increasing them to market value. The receiving corporation must record the assets at market value if the transferor is a foreign corporation. The value at which the receiving corporation records the assets constitutes, for the transferor, the acquisition costs of the shares received. If the receiving corporation does not continue the book value, the difference constitutes an immediately taxable gain for the transferor. If the transferor is a corporation, the gain is subject to corporation income tax at the regular rates. If he is an individual or a partnership, the gain is taxed at the lower rates applicable to capital gains, namely, at half of the taxpayer's regular income tax rate.

In order to induce sole proprietors and partnerships to merge their businesses into corporations, such mergers are excepted from real estate acquisition tax when the mergers are resolved before December 31, 1981.

The Law contains specific provisions to prevent application of the tax benefits if, as a result of the merger, the heretofore existing codetermination by labor is reduced.

Liquidation

During the liquidation stage, which shall as a rule not exceed three years, any hidden reserves accumulated by the corporation during its lifetime will be dissolved and taxed. However, the income tax paid by the corporation is available as a tax credit to the resident shareholder.

The great attraction of the

GmbH & Co. KG

to German investors is due to the fact that it combines the advantage of overall limited liability under civil law with the advantage of being taxed as a partnership instead of as a corporation. Taxwise the partnership's profit attributable to the limited partner accrues directly to him without having first been exposed to corporation income tax. Similarily the partnership's loss attributable to the limited partner likewise accrues directly to him, but without the limited partner being obliged to absorb such loss, as he would be obliged if there were an *Organschaft* type of profit and loss pooling between him and a corporation. For the foreign partner, however, there is no such advantage as he must always pay the flat rate of 50 per cent. If the foreign partner holds the investment through a German corporate subsidiary the direct accrual of the partnership's loss may be of advantage as it can be set-off against other income of the subsidiary. But apart therefrom the subsidiary is taxed for its share of the partnership's profit at the corporation income tax rate, and the foreign parent is in no better position, taxwise, than it would be if the partnership were a corporate subsidiary.

130

Taxation of Foreign Corporations

Foreign corporations are subject to German corporation income tax on their income derived from German sources only if they either maintain a permanent establishment in Germany or if their income falls into one of the classes of income defined as non-resident income from German sources.

Non-resident income from German sources is basically classified as:

income from farming and forestry carried on within Germany;

business income from a permanent establishment or permanent representative maintained within Germany, business income from own or chartered ships or aircraft operating between German ports and between German and foreign ports, unless the foreign state in which the enterprise has its place of management exempts corresponding income of German resident tax payers likewise from taxation, and income from the sale of a substantial participation in a German corporation;

income from capital investments, in particular dividends and constructive dividends;

income from capital reductions and liquidations unless the repayment of earlier capital contributions is involved;

income of silent partners;

interest income when the loan is secured by a mortgage on German real estate, or when the loan is registered in a German public debt record *(Schuldbuch)*, or when the loan constitutes a bond issue of a German borrower, in which case the so-called coupon tax applies;
rental and royalty income from German real estate or from industrial property rights registered in Germany;

income from know-how licence agreements or technical assistance agreements;

income from leasing machinery and equipment to German lessees;

income from the sale of German real estate within two years after purchase.

If one of these conditions is met, the respective income is subject to German corporation income tax unless the provisions of one of the many tax conventions exclude Germany's right to impose taxes.

As can be seen from the above listing, the following important types of income from German sources are not subject to German income taxes:

income from export sales made to Germany;

interest income from normal commercial loans to German borrowers unsecured by a mortgage on German real estate.

In the cases where an income tax liability exists because the income qualifies as non-resident income from German sources, the tax rate is 50 per cent unless the rate is reduced by a tax convention. With respect to dividend income, interest income, royalty income and income as a silent partner, however, the tax liability is discharged by the 25 per cent withholding tax withheld at source.

Service on Foreign Corporations

The German tax authorities may request that foreign corporations which are liable for German taxes appoint a German representative who is authorized to receive tax documents for the foreign corporation. If the foreign corporation fails to make such appointment, any tax document is deemed served upon the foreign corporation when deposited with the German post regardless of whether it is actually received by the foreign corporation or not.

Permanent Establishment *(Betriebsstätte)*

German tax law does contain definitions of what constitutes a permanent establishment, but, in view of the numerous tax conventions concluded by Germany, it seems more appropriate to quote here the definition of a permanent establishment contained in one of the more recent conventions namely, the Convention between the United States and Germany, which follows, to a great extent, the OECD draft double-taxation convention:

"(c) (aa) The term "permanent establishment" means a fixed place of business in which the business of an enterprise of one of the contracting States is wholly or partly carried on.

(bb) A permanent establishment shall include especially:
a place of management;
a branch;
an office;
a store or other sales outlet;
a factory;
a workshop;
a mine, quarry or other place of extraction of natural resources;
a building site or construction or assembly project which exists for more than twelve months.

(cc) Notwithstanding subparagraph (c) (aa) of this paragraph a permanent establishment shall be deemed not to include one or more of the following activities:

the use of facilities for the purpose of storage, display or delivery of goods or merchandise belonging to the enterprise;

the maintenance of a stock of goods or merchandise belonging to the enterprise for the purpose of storage, display or delivery;

the maintenance of a stock of goods or merchandise belonging to the enterprise for the purpose of processing by another enterprise;

the maintenance of a fixed place of business for the purpose of purchasing goods or merchandise, or for collecting information, for the enterprise;

the maintenance of a fixed place of business for the purpose of advertising, for the supply of information, for scientific research or for similar activities, if they have a preparatory or auxiliary character, for the enterprise.

(dd) Even if an enterprise of one of the contracting States does not have a permanent establishment in the other State under subparagraph (c) (aa) to (cc) of this paragraph, nevertheless it shall be deemed to have a permanent establishment in the latter State if it is engaged in trade or business in that State through an agent who has authority to conclude contracts in the name of the enterprise and regularly exercises that authority in that State, unless the exercise of authority is limited to the purchase of goods or merchandise for the account of the enterprise.

(ee) An enterprise of one of the contracting States shall not be deemed to have a permanent establishment in the other State merely because it is engaged in trade or business in that other State through a broker, general commission agent or any other agent of an independent status, where such person is acting in the ordinary course of business.

(ff) The fact that a resident or a corporation of one of the contracting States controls, is controlled by, or is under common control with (i) a corporation of the other State or (ii) a corporation which engages in trade or business in that other State (whether through a permanent establishment or otherwise) shall not be taken into account in determining whether such resident or corporation has a permanent establishment in that other State."

In addition to the above definition of a permanent establishment, it should be noted that a foreign corporation is always deemed to have a permanent establishment in Germany when it participates as a partner in a German partnership, be it as a general partner or a limited partner. The consequence can be avoided, however, if the foreign corporation holds such investment through a German corporate subsidiary.

The taxable income

of a permanent establishment will, as a rule, be determined in the same manner as if it were an independent German corporation. Its income is thus the difference between the net worth of the permanent establishment at the end of the fiscal year and the net worth at the end of the preceding fiscal year, all as shown in the books which are to be kept by the permanent establishment within Germany.

While the income of the permanent establishment derived from dealing with third parties presents no problem, it is different with respect to the dealings between the permanent establishment and its foreign headquarters. These dealings must be at arm's length, similarly to the arm's length dealings of a German corporation with its shareholders. If this is the case, the transactions will be recognized.

The principle is clearly set forth in the tax convention between the United States and Germany, which reads as follows:

"where an enterprise of one of the contracting States is engaged in trade or business in the other State through a permanent establishment situated therein, there shall be attributed to such permanent establishment the industrial or commercial profits which it might be expected to derive if it were an independent enterprise engaged in the same or similar activities under the same or similar conditions and dealing at arm's length with the enterprise of which it is a permanent establishment."

However the tax authorities hold the disputed view that this does not apply to interest or royalty charged by the foreign headquarters to the permanent establishment.

The so determined profits of the permanent establishment are subject to corporation income tax at the flat rate of 50 per cent regardless of whether the profit is retained or remitted to the foreign headquarters. This tax disadvantage over the taxation of a subsidiary company is the reason why most foreign operations in Germany are carried on in the form of a subsidiary company. In case the permanent establishment has no income, which is particularly true of the representative or liaison offices of banks, the tax authorities will, as a rule, consider a certain percentage of the office's expenses as profit.

Double Taxation Conventions

restrict to some extent the definition of a permanent establishment contained in internal German law, but their practical effect lies more in excluding German taxation of non-resident income from German sources altogether or reducing the same. Thus it is a common feature of the modern German tax conventions that Germany's right to tax interest and royalty income is excluded. This income is taxed only in the country where the lender or licensor is domiciled. The same applies to income derived from the sale of a substantial participation in a German corporation. Furthermore, some conventions reduce the withholding tax on dividends from 25 per cent to a lower rate such as 15 or 20 per cent. A 15 per cent rate is for instance provided in the convention between the United States and Germany. Under that convention, however, the full withholding tax of 25 per cent is payable when more than 7.5 per cent of the dividend received by the US corporation is either directly or indirectly reinvested by it in the German corporation within the calendar year preceding the year in which the transfer was made, the calendar year of the transfer or in the following calendar year. In this event the withholding tax of 25 per cent is payable on the amount of the reinvested dividend. In view of the fact that the 1977 tax reform has increased the corporation income tax rate for distributed earnings from an effective rate of 24.5 per cent to 36 per cent and has excluded foreign shareholders from the tax credit, it is expected that by renegotiations of the terms of the conventions the negative impact of the tax reform on foreign shareholders may, at least to some extent be mitigated by reducing the withholding tax.

The TRADE TAX *(Gewerbesteuer)*

is a federal tax, like the corporation income tax, but it is administered to some extent by the municipalities. The basic tax rates are set by federal statutes and a factor determined by each municipality is applied to the basic rate. The tax is imposed on all business carried on in Germany, including liaison offices and permanent establishments of foreign corporations. The tax is based on profit and capital and, in addition, at the option of the municipality, on payroll. The basis for the

trade tax on income

is the determination made for income tax purposes which is adjusted by certain additions and deductions. The more important ones are:

Additions:

> interest paid on long-term debts, generally loans for a term of more than one year;

> the profit share of the silent partner, unless the silent partner himself is liable for the trade tax on the profit share, which condition is not met in the case of foreign silent partners;

137

one-half of rental or royalty payments under lease agreements for the use of property other than real estate, unless the lessor or licensor himself is liable for the trade tax on income.

This condition is not met in the case of foreign lessors and licensors. The addition is, however, not made in the case of know-how or patent license agreements since they are not considered as "lease" agreements.

losses from a partnership;

charitable contributions, except those for scientific purposes.

Deductions:

1.2 per cent of the assessed value of real property located in Germany;

profits received from a partnership;

dividends received from a German or active foreign corporation, in which the tax payer held an interest of at least 25 per cent;

the profit share of a silent partner;

rental or royalties received for the use of property other than real estate, to the extent that the lessee was not permitted to deduct such payments;

profits allocable to a foreign permanent establishment;

operating losses, including a loss carry-forward.

The basis for the

trade tax on capital

is the value of the business as determined for purposes of the net worth tax, which is again subject to certain adjustments. The more important ones are:

138

Additions:

long-term debts which have been deducted for purposes of the net worth tax;

the addition is again not made in the case of know-how or patent licence agreements;

the value of rented or licensed property other than real estate. The addition, however, is not to be made when the property is included in the lessor's or licensor's trade capital, except when an entire business or a separate division having a value of more than DM 2.5 million has been leased.

Deductions:

the assessed value of real estate owned;

the value of a partnership interest;

the interest in a German or active foreign corporation, provided the interest amounts to at least 25 per cent of the share capital (intercorporate privilege, *Schachtelprivileg*);

the value of the assets allocated to a foreign permanent establishment.

Trade tax on payroll

is assessed on the gross monthly or quarterly payroll. It is not levied in all municipalities, and it is presently discussed to abolish this tax altogether.

Trade tax rates

As the municipalities determine the factor to be applied to the basic rates set forth in the statute, no precise rates can be given. Trade tax on income ranges from approximately 12 to 17 per cent, on capital from approcimately 0.4 to 0.8 per cent and on payroll from approximately 1 to 2 per cent. However, since trade tax is a deductible expense not only for income tax but also for trade tax purposes, the actual tax burden is considerably lower than these rates would suggest. An income of up to DM 15 000,– and a capital of up to DM 6000,– is exempt from trade tax.

Summary

Summary of Corporation Income and Trade Income Tax Burden of a German subsidiary and of a German Branch of a US Corporation.

1) Subsidiary with full profit distribution

Assumed net income before income tax		1,000,000
Less trade tax on income at approximately 16%		(160,000)
		840,000
Less corporation income tax at 56% of 840,000		(470,400)
		369,600
Add: reduction of tax to arrive at 36% rate, 5/11 of 369,600		168,000
Dividend		537,600

Alternative 1:

Less dividend withholding tax at 15% of 537,600 in case of no-reinvestment	80,640	
Net dividend		456,960

Total tax burden: 54,3%

Alternative 2:

Less: dividend withholding tax at 23,5% of 537,600 (mixed rate) in case of reinvestment of more than 7,5% of dividend received	126,336	
Net dividend		411,264

Total tax burden: 58,8%

2) Subsidiary with full retention
   of profit   1,000,000
   Assumed net income before income taxes
   Less trade tax on income
   at approximately 16%   (160,000)
                                                 ─────────
                                                  840,000

   Less corporation income tax at 56%   (470,400)
                                                 ─────────
                                                  369,600

   Total tax burden: 63,0%

3) Branch
   Assumed net income before income taxes   1,000,000
   Less trade tax on income
   at approximately 16%   160,000
                                                  ─────────
                                                   840,000

   Less corporation income tax at 50%
   regardless of whether income is
   retained or remitted to home office   420,000
                                                  ─────────
   income after taxes   420,000

Total tax burden: 58,0%

Summary of tax burden expressed in per cent

Subsidiary with full distribution and no reinvestment   54,3%
Subsidiary with full distribution and reinvestment   58,8%
Subsidiary with full retention of profit   63,0%
Branch regardless of remittance or retention   58,0%

141

Formula to determine maximum dividend distribution:

$$\frac{\text{taxable income minus (non-deductible expenses} \times 2{,}2727)}{1{,}5625}$$

Non deductible expenses are among others: net worth tax and one half of the compensation paid to the members of a Supervisory Board.

NET WORTH TAX *(Vermögensteuer)*

Germany imposes an annual net worth tax. Since January 1, 1978 the rates are 0,7 per cent for corporations and 0,5 per cent for individuals. The tax is not deductible, also not for individuals. However, individuals enjoy an exemption of DM 70 000,– from the tax. German corporations are subject to the tax on all their assets, domestic and foreign. The valuation of the assets is made in accordance with the provisions of the Valuation Law *(Bewertungsgesetz)* which provides, inter alia, that German real estate property is valued at its assessed value (tax value = *Einheitswert*). As a rule, the tax value is considerably lower than market value. Liabilities are deducted from the assets; also shareholders' loans substituting for capital are deductible. The intercorporate privilege *(Schachtelprivileg)*, is still relevant in the field of net worth tax. A German corporation which holds 25 per cent or more of the shares of another German corporation, may treat this participation as exempt from net worth tax, provided it has held the participation for at least 12 months.

Foreign corporations are subject to German net worth tax only upon certain of their German assets as defined in the Valuation Law, namely:

German agricultural and forestry property;
German real property;
German business assets, such as the assets of a permanent establishment in Germany;
participations of at least 25 per cent in the share capital of a German corporation;
industrial property registered in a German register;

other assets leased or licensed to a German enterprise, including know-how or trademarks;

mortgages or other charges secured by German real estate or German ships; and

claims of a silent partner against a German debtor.

unless such taxation is excluded by one of the many double taxation conventions.

A somewhat comparable tax which recurs annually is the

MUNICIPAL REAL PROPERTY TAX *(Grundsteuer)*

levied on the tax value of land and buildings located in Germany. The rates vary depending on the municipality and the class of property and range between about 0.5 per cent and 2.5 per cent.

PERSONAL INCOME TAX *(Einkommensteuer)*

The world-wide income of persons domiciled in or residing in Germany for more than six months is subject to this tax, provided the income is derived from certain categories and further provided the right to taxation is not excluded by a tax convention. The seven categories defined by the income tax law are: income from agriculture or forestry, from business, from professional services, from employment, from capital investment, from rentals, and from specially listed sources such as annuities. Income which does not fall within these categories is tax free. Under certain conditions an individual "without income" may, however, be taxed upon an estimated income based upon his apparent living expenses.

The income of individual businessmen is generally determined in accordance with the same rules explained above with respect to corporations. The income of individuals deriving income from employment is computed by deducting from gross income the expenses incurred in producing or preserving such income. Individual taxpayers are entitled to claim certain blanket deductions and certain special deductions. Individual taxpayers are further allowed to deduct from their income the church taxes paid. The individual's income is taxed at progressive rates which range from 22 per cent in the lowest bracket – DM 3,329.– to DM 16,000.– to 56 per cent in the highest bracket which starts at DM 130,000.–. Due to the blanket deductions available, however, the actual tax burden is other than the percentage would indicate. Taxation starts with an annual income of DM 3,359.– the tax then being DM 6.– or the equivalent of 0,19 per cent. Married couples are entitled to file a joint return with the consequence that the taxable income is split and the resultant tax doubled.

For income from Berlin sources, the assessed income tax liability is reduced by 30 per cent. Employees in Berlin receive, in addition to this tax allowance, a tax free supplementary payment according to their income bracket. The supplementary payment is made out of the wage tax withheld by the employer.

Capital Gains

The treatment of capital gains of individuals is quite complex. As regards capital gains from the sale of business assets the same rules apply as in the case of a corporation, i. e. such gains are fully taxable except when an exemption is obtained by proper reinvestment. In certain cases the tax rate is reduced to one half of the regular rate, namely in the case of gains from the sale of a business as a whole or a division thereof, from the sale of all of the shares of a corporation, from the liquidation of a business, from the sale of a partnership interest in whole or in part and from the liquidation of a partnership. Losses in all these cases reduce the taxable income.

As regards non-business assets, gains or losses from a sale neither increase nor reduce the taxable income, except for the following: Gains or losses from the sale of real estate within two years after acquisition and from the sale of other assets, in particular securities within six months after acquisition are taxable income. The gain from such sale is taxable at the full rate. The gain or loss from the sale of shares in a corporation is taxable income, provided the seller, during the preceding five years has held a substantial participation (*wesentliche Beteiligung*) in the company and sells during a fiscal year more than 1 per cent of the company's capital. A substantial participation is a participation of more than 25 per cent. The gain on such sale is taxed at half the regular tax rate only, the maximum tax rate therefore is 28 per cent.

Wage tax withholding

In the case of income from employment, the income tax is called wage tax *(Lohnsteuer)* and the employer is liable for withholding the tax and remitting the same to the tax office. The employee need only file a tax return when his annual income exceeds DM 24,000.–. In practice, the tax administration requires the withholding of the tax also by foreign employers which employ persons in Germany under conditions which are not sufficient to constitute a permanent establishment of the employer under the applicable tax convention.

Stock options

are not common in Germany. German corporations may permit their employees to purchase the corporation's shares below the market price. The difference between the market price and the price the employee has to pay does not constitute taxable income, provided the employee has agreed not to dispose of the stock for a period of five years and the difference does not exceed DM 500.– per calendar year.

Non-resident individuals

are taxed when their income falls within one of the categories of non-resident income from German sources or when professional services or services of an employee are rendered in Germany or the result of such services is destined to directly benefit the German economy. However, this principle is greatly mitigated by the tax conventions for non-residents working in Germany less than six months. For example the tax convention between the United States and Germany contains a rather typical provision in this respect:

"Compensation for labor or personal services (including compensation derived from the practice of a liberal profession and the rendering of services as a director) performed in the Federal Republic by a resident of the United States shall be exempt from tax by the Federal Republic if

(a) he is present in the Federal Republic for a period or periods not exceeding a total of 183 days during a taxable year,

(b) such labor or personal services are performed as an employee of, or under contract with, a resident or corporation or other entity of the United States and such compensation is borne by such resident or corporation or other entity, and

(c) such compensation is not borne by a permanent establishment which such resident or corporation or other entity has in the Federal Republic."

Lump sum taxation *(Pauschbesteuerung)*

Foreign nationals who are subject to German taxation and who bring special skills to the German economy which are not or only to a lesser degree available in Germany (such as scientists, university professors, engineers, artists, and in very exceptional cases also businessmen) may request that their income and net worth tax liability is assessed in a lump sum or that the otherwise applicable tax rates be adequately reduced. The highest tax authority of each state will decide, in its discretion, on such requests with the consent of the Federal Ministry of Finance. Concessions are, as a rule, not granted for longer than three years even though they could legally be granted for ten years.

XVI. CUSTOMS

Products imported into the Federal Republic of Germany from a country which is neither a member of the EEC nor a member of EFTA are subject to customs duty, while products imported from an EEC member state or an EFTA member state and having originated therein are no longer subject thereto. Special regulations exist, however, with respect to agricultural products. Trade between the Federal Republic of Germany and the "German Democratic Republic" (East Germany) is still treated as "German" domestic trade. The duty rates are set forth in the

COMMON MARKET JOINT CUSTOMS TARIFF,

so that the same rates apply regardless where a product enters the Common Market.

The rates depend on the classification of the products, which is likewise set forth in the Common Market Joint Customs Tariff. The customs authorities will, on request, give advance rulings with respect to the classification of products.

The duty is payable on the "normal value" of the products imported as the same is defined in the

COMMON MARKET JOINT CUSTOMS
EVALUATION ORDINANCE

It provides:

"For the application of the joint customs tariff the customs value of any imported goods shall be taken to be the normal price, that is to say, the price which they would fetch at the time when the duty becomes payable on a sale made under conditions of free competition between buyer and seller independent of each other (normal price)

the normal price of any imported goods shall be determined on the following assumptions:

that the goods are treated as having been delivered to the buyer at the place of introduction into the customs area of the Community;
and
that the seller will bear all costs, incidental to the sale and to the delivery of the goods to the place of importation and that they are accordingly included in the normal price;

but

that the buyer will bear any duties or taxes payable in the customs area of the Community and that they are accordingly not included in the normal price".

The application of this provision will lead to an adjustment of the invoice price whenever the same does not comply with this rule. For example, the invoice price is too low because portions of the price have artificially been split off and are paid under a different designation, such as patent and trademark royalties, or certain advertising expenses are shifted to the importer or a subsidiary is subsidized during its start-up period by obtaining lower purchase prices. The adjustment is done by adding a certain percentage to the invoice price and by applying the customs rate then to this increased invoice price. This is comparable to the profit adjustment made by the tax authorities when a hidden profit distribution is assumed and the amount of the same imputed to the company as profit. The decisions of the customs authorities may well differ from those of the tax authorities, on the one hand producing higher duties and at the same time resulting in higher taxes on the other hand. As customs duties are defined to constitute taxes under German law decisions by the customs authorities are appealable to the tax courts.

XVII. FOREIGN TRADE AND EXCHANGE CONTROL

The regulatory basis for Germany's foreign trade in the widest sense – exports and imports, services, payments and capital transactions – is the Foreign Trade Law *(Außenwirtschaftsgesetz, AWG)*.
The *AWG* establishes the general principle of freedom of foreign trade. However, as a "skeleton law", it sets forth a number of authorizations for the government to regulate foreign trade by imposing restrictions and introducing reporting requirements.

IMPORTS

included in the so-called "import list" do not require a license. The only restriction contained in the *AWG* itself is that imports excluded from the import list do require a license. Presently, however, practically all imports from non-communist countries are included in the import list.

RESTRICTIONS

Apart therefrom, the *AWG* merely sets forth the conditions under which the government is authorized to impose further restrictions. The government may prescribe by ordinance that under certain conditions specified transactions or acts either require a license or are prohibited altogether. The scope of such restrictions must be limited as much as possible so that interference with the freedom of business can be kept to a minimum. Restrictions imposed must, therefore, be removed as soon as the reasons justifying their imposition are no longer valid.
The *AWG* distinguishes between two sets of conditions, one which may be imposed on transactions in general and the other dealing with specific transactions only. Restrictions may be imposed on

transactions in general

only for one of the following reasons:

to meet obligations under Germany's international treaties;

to protect against damaging effects on the German economy resulting from measures taken abroad which restrain, distort or prevent competition within Germany or which result in a restraint of trade with the foreign country;

to safeguard the security and the foreign relations of Germany.

So far the government has invoked the authority to impose such restrictions only to a very limited extent.

Among

specific transactions

the following may be restricted:

exports, when the restriction is necessary to safeguard the indispensable domestic supply of products;

imports qualifying for the general license by their inclusion in the aforementioned "import list", as far as their delivery time is concerned;

services, mainly to protect specified branches of German industry.

The number of restrictions presently in effect is rather limited. They concern e.g. agricultural exports into non-Common Market countries. Agreements on extended delivery times of generally licensed imports require a license.

FREE CONVERTIBILITY

The *Deutsche Mark* has been freely convertible into other currencies since 1958.

150

EXPORT OF CAPITAL

If necessary for the restoration of the German balance of payments, the following transactions between residents and non-residents may be restricted:

the purchase of foreign real estate or of rights with respect to such real estate;

the purchase by residents of foreign securities;

the purchase by residents of bills of exchange issued or accepted by non-residents;

the keeping of banking accounts by residents with foreign banks outside of Germany;

the granting of loans or other credits and payment facilities to non-residents.

If necessary to prevent or counteract substantial detrimental effects on the German capital market, the public offering within Germany of bearer or order bonds issued by non-residents and providing for the payment of a certain sum of money may be restricted.

To date, none of these restrictions of capital export has been imposed.

A number of important forms of capital exports are not even mentioned as being potentially subject to restrictions, in particular, the repatriation of money invested in Germany and the payment of dividends to foreign recipients, the establishment of German branches or subsidiaries abroad and the participation in foreign enterprises.

IMPORT OF CAPITAL

Transactions between residents and non-residents may be restricted when they relate to:

the purchase by non-residents of real estate within Germany or of rights with respect to such real estate;

151

the purchase by non-residents of ships registered in a German ship register or of a right with respect to such ship;

the purchase by non-residents of enterprises having their domicile in Germany or of interests in such enterprises;

the purchase by non-residents of German securities;

the purchase by non-residents of bills of exchange issued or accepted by residents;

the taking up by residents of loans or other credit or payment facilities and the sale of receivables by residents to non-residents;

the keeping of and the interest payment on banking accounts of non-residents with banks within Germany.

In addition, the following may be restricted:

the formation of enterprises having their domicile within Germany by non-residents or with the participation of non-residents;

the provision of assets by non-residents for enterprises, branches and permanent establishments within Germany.

Such restrictions of capital imports may be imposed to counteract a decrease in the purchasing power of the *Deutsche Mark* or to safeguard Germany's balance of payments.

The government invoked this authorization on several occasions. The following

RESTRICTIONS

are presently in effect:

Without a license non-residents may not purchase from residents:

- treasury bills;
- non-interest bearing treasury notes;
- governmental food storage agency bills;

- bills of exchange endorsed by a German bank, drawn on a resident and payable within Germany, and bills of exchange issued by a resident and endorsed by a German bank;
- bills of exchange issued by a resident and accepted by a German bank;
- German bearer or order bonds maturing within four years or with the obligation of the resident to repurchase them within four years.

The license required in all such cases is, as a matter of policy, never granted.

A further restriction to be mentioned in this context is the so-called coupon tax introduced in 1965 which is levied on interest payments to non-resident holders of German bonds. This restriction is likewise aimed against the influx of "hot money" into Germany.

The much discussed

BARDEPOT (Cash Deposit)

introduced early in 1972 which is presently no longer in effect, did not prevent German residents from borrowing outside of Germany nor did it introduce any license requirement for such borrowing but it substantially increased the cost of any foreign borrowing. Resident borrowers – including German branches and subsidiaries of foreign enterprises – had to deposit in an interest free account with the Federal Bank a certain portion of any direct or indirect foreign borrowing. The rate to be so deposited was at first set at 40 per cent but was then raised to 50 per cent. It was levied on the aggregate monthly borrowing volume. When the Bardepot did not sufficiently reduce the import of foreign capital the government had to invoke its authorization to submit borrowings by residents from non-residents to prior approval.

153

VOID TRANSACTIONS

Wherever a license is required under the *AWG* for a transaction which is entered into without such a license, the transaction is null and void. It can be validated retroactively, however, by obtaining the license.

STATISTICS

The general freedom of foreign trade and the absence of licensing requirements is accompanied by a detailed reporting system which is used for statistical purposes and which allows the authorities to evaluate the impact of foreign trade on the national economy and to determine whether license requirements need be introduced or not.

TRADE WITH EAST GERMANY,

with the "German Democratic Republic" (DDR), formerly called interzonal trade, is not treated as foreign trade with the EEC but still as inter–German trade with considerable advantages of the DDR (saving of duties, interest–free accumulated debts from West-German imports). COMECON is not considered by the West as an economic organization comparable to EEC, and EEC accordingly refuses multilateral trade agreements with COMECON. A point of dispute is also the separate privileged status of DDR.

The basis of decisions of the West German authorities with regard to trade with East Germany is still the post-war regulation of the Allied Military Governments. The trade with other Eastern bloc countries remains on a bilateral basis. Imports from such countries are quasi liberalized wherever long term trade agreements with Germany exist. As a rule, licenses for Eastern imports are freely granted.

TABLE OF SELECTED CODES AND STATUTES*

Constitutional Law

Grundgesetz für die Bundesrepublik Deutschland (Constitution of the Federal Republik of Germany) — GG

Courts and Procedure

Gerichtsverfassungsgesetz (Law on Organisation of Courts) — GVG

Zivilprozeßordnung (Code of Civil Procedure) — ZPO

Konkursordnung (Bankruptcy Law) — KO

Vergleichsordnung (Law on Composition Procedure) — VerglO

Zwangsversteigerungsgesetz (Law on Compulsory Sale of Real Estate) — ZVG

Arbeitsgerichtsgesetz (Labor Court Law) — ArbGG

Verwaltungsgerichtsordnung (Administrative Courts and Procedure) — VwGO

Private and Commercial Law

Bürgerliches Gesetzbuch (Civil Code) — BGB

Handelsgesetzbuch (Commercial Code) — HGB

Aktiengesetz (Stock Corporation Law) — AktG

---

* Except where otherwise indicated references are to federal law.

GmbH-Gesetz	*GmbHG*
Umwandlungsgesetz (Law on Mergers)	*UmwG*
Publizitätsgesetz (Law on Disclosure Requirements for large Enterprises)	*PublG*
Wechselgesetz (Law on Bills of Exchange)	*WG*
Scheckgesetz (Law on Cheques)	*ScheckG*
Kreditwesengesetz (Banking Law)	*KWG*
Gesetz über Kapitalanlage-gesellschaften (Mutual Funds Law)	*KAGG*
Auslandsinvestmentgesetz (Law on Foreign Investment Shares)	*AuslInvestmG*
Gesetz über allgemeine Geschäftsbedingungen (Law on General Business Conditions)	*ABGG*
Gesetz gegen unlauteren Wettbewerb (Fair Trade Law)	*UWG*
Gesetz gegen Wettbewerbs-beschränkungen (Cartel Law)	*GWB*
Rabattgesetz (Law on Rebates)	*RabattG*
Zugabe-Verordnung (Gifts Regulation)	*ZugabeVO*
Patentgesetz (Patent Law)	*PatG*
Warenzeichengesetz (Trademark Law)	*WZG*

Gebrauchsmustergesetz	*GebrMG*
(Law on Utility Models)	
Geschmacksmustergesetz	*GeschmG*
(Law on Commercial Designs)	
Urheberrechtsgesetz	*UrhG*
(Copyright Law)	
Verlagsgesetz	*VerlG*
(Law on Publishing)	
Gewerbeordnung	*GewO*
(Law on Trades)	

Labor Law

Kündigungsschutzgesetz	*KSchG*
Angestelltenkündigungsschutzgesetz	
(Laws on Termination of Employees)	
Arbeitnehmererfindergesetz	*ArbnErfG*
(Law on Employee Inventions)	
Betriebsverfassungsgesetz	*BVerfG*
(Shop Constitution Law)	
Mitbestimmungsgesetz	*MitbestG*
(Co-Determination Law)	

Tax Law

Abgabeordnung	*AO*
(Basic Tax Code)	
Steueranpassungsgesetz	*StAnpG*
(Tax Adjustment Law)	
Bewertungsgesetz	*BewG*
(Valuation Law)	
Einkommensteuergesetz	*EStG*
(Income Tax Law)	
Körperschaftssteuergesetz	*KStG*
(Corporation Income Tax Law)	

Gewerbesteuergesetz (Trade Tax Law)	*GewStG*
Vermögensteuergesetz (Net Worth Tax Law)	*VStG*
Kapitalverkehrsteuergesetz (Capital Investment Tax Law)	*KVStG*
Umsatzsteuergesetz – *Mehrwertsteuergesetz* (Turnover Tax Law – Added Value Tax)	*UStG*
Grunderwerbsteuergesetz (Real Estate Acquisition Tax Law) and amending statutes of the states	*GrEStG*
Wechselsteuergesetz (Bills of Exchange Tax Law)	*WStG*
Zollgesetz (Customs Law)	*ZG*

Foreign Trade

Außenwirtschaftsgesetz (Foreign Trade Law)	*AWG*

Aliens

Ausländergesetz (Law on Aliens)	*AuslG*

Penal Laws and Administrative Fines

Strafgesetzbuch (Penal Code)	*StGB*
Strafprozeßordnung (Code of Criminal Procedure)	*StPO*
Wirtschaftsstrafgesetz (Offences Relating to Business Matters)	*WiStG*
Ordnungswidrigkeitengesetz (Administrative Offences)	*OWiG*

LIST OF SELECTED LAW JOURNALS (PERIODICALS)

All Fields of Law

Neue Juristische Wochenschrift	*NJW*

All Fields of Interest to Business

Betriebsberater	*BB*
Der Betrieb	*DB*

Foreign Law and Conflict of Laws

Rabels Zeitschrift für ausländisches und internationales Privatrecht	*RabelsZ*

Corporations

Die Aktiengesellschaft	*AG*
GmbH Rundschau	*GmbHRdsch*

Banks and Securities

Wertpapiermitteilungen part IV	*WM*

Trade Practices

Wettbewerb in Recht und Praxis	*WRP*
Wirtschaft und Wettbewerb	*WuW*

Industrial Property Rights

Gewerblicher Rechtsschutz und Urheberrecht with international section	*GRUR*

Taxes

Deutsches Steuerrecht	*DStR*
Umsatzsteuer-Rundschau	*UStR*

Foreign Trade

Außenwirtschaftsdienst	*AWD*

INDEX [1]

---

[1] References are to pages. Matters dealing with taxes will be found under a detailed tax index p. 171.

168

169

Taxes (separate index)